DIAMONDS

DIAMONDS

EIGHT KEY QUALITIES
THAT OPEN THE DOOR
TO THE SPLENDOR OF LIVING

BY
**DON KLASSEN AND ARTHUR GORDON
AND BILL HARTFIEL**

Century Communications

Published by: Century Communications
14472 Wilds Parkway
Prior Lake, Minnesota 55372
Telephone 612-445-9082

3 Newlands Business Park, Nass Road
Dublin, Ireland.
Telephone 353-1-459950

Design by: Robert Aulicino, Pro-Art Graphic Design

Printed by: Friesens, Altona, Manitoba, Canada ROG OBO

Ordering Information:

Quantity Sales: This book is available at special quantity discounts when purchased in bulk by
businesses, organizations, associations, libraries, schools and others. Please write to:
Century Communications
14472 Wilds Parkway
Prior Lake, Minnesota 55372
Telephone: 952-445-9082
Fax: 952-445-9194

U.S. and International trade bookstores may order from:
The Bookmen, Inc.
525 North 3rd Street
Minneapolis, Minnesota 55401
Telephone: 612-359-5959 or 800-328-8411
Fax: 612-341-2903 or 800-266-5636

ISBN: 0-9676553-0-7

Library of Congress: 99-068479

DIAMONDS

FOREWORD

Every one of our fellow passengers on this space-ship Earth has the potential to make a real difference with their lives. But many people, for many reasons, never realize that potential. It remains locked inside.

Then, on the other hand, there are some whose lives glow with energy and purpose. They set goals and achieve them, rebound from setbacks, are not daunted by obstacles, and make a lasting and healing impact on their surroundings. We call these people Diamonds.

Where do diamonds come from? In their original state, actual diamonds have little appeal to the eye. They look like cloudy pebbles or dingy rocks. It takes hours of work by a skilled craftsman to bring out the hidden beauty. But when the diamond cutter's exacting standards are met, and the polished stone is placed in the right setting, the result is a treasure that outlasts a lifetime.

Is there a parallel between the evolution of a natural jewel and the emergence of an individual who comes to be regarded as one of the Diamonds in the ranks of humanity? The writers of this book think there is—a very strong parallel.

In researching this book, we identified eight key qualities common to Diamonds of the human kind. We have written a chapter on each of them, with the first letters of these qualities forming our acronym, Diamonds.

We are sure of one thing. We believe that these key qualities can be acquired, not instantly perhaps but gradually, by any dedicated person who studies them, learns from them and applies them to their own situation. Such a process need not be complicated or tiresome. It can be stimulating, rewarding and fun. It is an internal progression—and a lifelong one.

In the pages that follow you will find many examples of people who have earned the right to be called Diamonds. Several of them appear more than once, but important as these characters are, the most important person is the reader—you.

CONTENTS

THE EIGHT KEY QUALITIES

DESIRE

A sustained passion for reaching a certain goal or goals.

"It seems that intense desire creates not only its own opportunities, but its own talents."
-Eric Hoffer-

Have you ever had glimpses of a mysterious law that can occasionally move in and take charge of human affairs? That law can be expressed like this: when we want something badly enough, people and circumstances come into our lives to help turn dreams into realities.

It is also evident that the law operates under one strict condition: the person who benefits from it first must have achieved a special state of mind. He or she must be driven by desire, by which we mean an enduring and passionate longing to reach a certain goal or goals.

1

Note that word passionate. Wistful daydreaming won't activate the law. Unfocused ambitions won't do it. There has to be a sustained urgency. There needs to be an honest view of one's capabilities, as well as the unshakable belief that those capabilities can be strengthened and expanded.

This expansion, indeed, is one of the most remarkable features of the law. Once an individual attains the right mind-set, existing talents are enhanced. Not only that—new talents seem to appear out of nowhere.

The best way to see this law in operation is to look at the careers of people who clearly belong in the category of Diamonds. And we need to view them through a wide-angle lens, because once a state of intense desire takes hold, it impels its owner toward success in many areas and on many levels.

How did the authors of this book—two businessmen and a writer—set about finding such people? Here's a clue. Years ago a wise man, Russell Conwell, wrote a classic little story called: <u>Acres of Diamonds</u>. It tells of a man who spent his entire life searching far and wide for precious stones in remote places. He never found any because he never thought to look in his own back yard. That's where the diamonds were all the time, acres and acres of them.

The message of this fable is plain: whoever we are, wherever we live, there are Diamonds in our back yard waiting to be discovered, identified, studied, admired, and imitated. And this held true in our own case as we approached writing this book. To a large extent we found what we were seeking in our own back yard.

For two of us that back yard was the State of

Minnesota, and the Twin Cities area of Minneapolis and St. Paul where we live and work. Not only did we find some memorable individuals but also some outstanding companies. Chief among these was Medtronic, Inc., which in 1998 became the world's leading medical technology company as a result of a series of acquisitions.

Medtronic is a corporation led by some people, past and present, who clearly belong in the category of Diamonds and whose leadership has created a unique company culture. We will be referring frequently to Medtronic in the pages of this book because there is much to be learned from it both by business people and by citizens of every kind, wherever they live.

Let's begin, then, by considering the case of Kristine Johnson and her remarkable rise as President of two different divisions of Medtronic in the decade of the nineties.

The Diamonds of this world sparkle with energy and enthusiasm. So does dynamic, red- haired Kristine Johnson. She radiates an aura of confidence and exuberance. *"We all need an appetite for achievement,"* she says.

Kristine's eagerness to achieve was apparent even as an undergraduate at St. Olaf College in Northfield, Minnesota. Not content with majoring in one subject, she tackled three: mathematics, economics, and political science. After graduating she took a job in public relations with Cargill, the nation's largest privately held company. Cargill is a diversified international company that would have offered her many opportunities for advancement. Many people would have been satisfied with a staff position at a great company, but Kristine had a burning desire to be a line manager in a manufacturing company. She had the courage to make a change and was hired by Medtronic. Almost at once people in the company noticed her ability to work well with other people, her passion for excellence in everything she did, and her willingness to devote as much time and energy to a problem as its solution required.

In 1990 Kristine was named Vice President and General Manager of the Tachyarythmic Division for Medtronic. This division manufactures defibrillators, which are implantable devices that treat a heart condition characterized by rapid heartbeat. In its early stages of development, the Medtronic defibrillator met with all sorts of obstacles: law suits over patents, mechanical problems, uncertainty and delay where the required approval of the Federal Drug Administration was concerned. All these and countless other problems became the responsibility of Kristine Johnson. How well she succeeded in dealing with them is indicated by the fact that when she took the reins her division's revenues were only two and a half million dollars. Eight years later, in 1998, it was generating two hundred and sixty five million dollars.

All this called for sustained intense work; Kristine estimates that she works about fifty-five hours a week. *"But that's all right. I like being busy. I like a lot of activity."*

Of course, she does. Nothing is more satisfying than the sense of achievement that comes from doing a difficult job well.

There is another factor that kindles and sustains in people the kind of desire that leads to outstanding success in life. It's the feeling that one's efforts are making a real difference in the lives of other people.

At the heart of Kristine Johnson's desire is that kind of awareness. Even as she struggled with the early problems that beset Medtronic's defibrillator, she was convinced that ultimately it would help thousands of people find relief from pain and suffering and in many cases prolong their lives. And she was right: it has. The market for this product in recent years has grown 25% to 30% annually and in 1998 was 1.2 billion dollars world-wide.

Another trait that shines through the lives of Diamonds is a sense of proportion, of balance when it comes to judging the priorities of life. Kristine Johnson's job is of tremendous importance to her, but as a wife and the mother of two young girls, she knows that her family comes first. A few years ago she had an evening call from Nils Hasselmo who was then President of the University of Minnesota where Kristine served on the Foundation Board of Trustees. The call concerned matters of considerable importance to one of the largest learning institutions in the United States, but in the middle of it Kristine remembered that it was time to put her daughters to bed. *"I have to go now,"* she informed Hasselmo. *"I'm sorry, but it's the girls' bedtime."*

It is this ability to put first things first that characterizes everything Kristine Johnson does, and makes her such a valued member of the corporate team at Medtronic. She has a keenly analytical mind herself, but more important perhaps is her ability to train other people to concentrate their own analytical powers on one question or one problem and reach a solution without raising more and more questions or more and more problems. *"No one has unlimited energy,"* she says, *"and so we must put the energy we do have into what makes a difference."*

Steadfast in her commitment to her family, her church, and her community, strong in her knowledge of her own abilities and the support of her friends, Kristine Johnson is living her life and thoroughly enjoying it.

———————

Down through the years one trait seems to appear over and over again in the lives of people who eventually become Diamonds. It is the ability to overcome early adversity and through persistence and determination rise to great heights. There seems to be another invisible law that governs such people, the law of challenge-and-response. The greater the challenge, the more powerful the response. And desire is what sets this law in operation.

Go back over a century in American history to see an extraordinary example of this phenomenon. In 1862, during the troubled days of the Civil War, passengers on the Michigan railroad running between Port Huron and Detroit paid little attention to the shabbily-dressed fifteen year old who came through the cars selling newspapers and candies.

They knew him only as "Little Al". No one would have guessed that ultimately he would gain fame as "the man who invented the twentieth century." But that is what Thomas Alva Edison did.

Edison was a first-grade dropout who resolutely refused

to admit failure in any part of his life. His dream was to become an inventor, and he did not let his lack of formal education stop him. His great talent was to surround himself with the best possible engineers and scientists and to learn from all of them. Today he is remembered primarily for his three main inventions: the phonograph, the electric light bulb, and the motion-picture camera. By the time he died, he was credited with over a thousand patents. What is less well known is that he also conducted thousands of experiments that failed. But his discipline and desire to see things through to their completion never faltered. He had a vision of a splendid new world, not just for himself but for people everywhere; and to an amazing degree Edison made that dream came true.

Thomas Edison died in 1931. Even on his deathbed, his restless mind kept scanning possibilities, searching for things that would make the world a better place. At the very end, he shared one more glimpse of a future possibility. Awakening briefly from a coma, he looked at his wife Mina and murmured, *"It is very beautiful over there."*

Then he moved on and took his place in history.

It is rewarding to study the careers of those vibrant personalities who become the Diamonds of our society. It is also instructive to give some thought to those who never rise above mediocrity in the arena of life and to ask the critical question: why? Surely the non-achievers vastly outnumber the achievers. What is holding them back?

Very often, a basic problem is that they don't love their work. They may perform it adequately from day to day; they may be making a decent living and leading a reasonably happy life. But if they are honest, they admit that the thrill of solving problems is no longer there. The passion is gone, if indeed it ever existed. This means that on some deep fundamental level they are bored, and this boredom gradually erodes their confidence. They tell themselves that they have gone as far as they can go. The thought of a new challenge frightens them.

Almost always in such situations, individuals tend to underestimate themselves. They begin to put limits on their thinking. They may have potential skills, but they build a glass ceiling over them. "Oh", they lament, "I don't have enough education to try this, or enough experience to try that. Anyway, it's just too risky."

On the other hand, Diamonds' intense desire pushes these misgivings aside. This leaves them free to see the world as it might be, and gives them the vitality and confidence to drive toward that goal. Earl Nightingale, known to millions in his time for his popular radio program, "Our Changing World" wrote an essay in 1956 titled "The Strangest Secret". It received the first gold record ever awarded a spoken word message. In this recording, Nightingale offered a memorable definition. "Success," he said, "is the progressive realization of a worthy ideal." Diamonds know how to take the necessary steps in that progression. Less determined people do not. Yet success by this definition is open to the teacher, the gas station owner, the researcher or whoever is doing a job that they enthusiastically want to do.

Sometimes this pursuit of a worthy ideal leads Diamonds into totally new fields of endeavor. Here they do not fear the risks or challenges, because they know that the same dynamics that brought them success in the past can also serve them well in their new surroundings.

This truth blazes forth in the life-story of an eighty nine year old Minnesotan, Elmer Andersen, today one of the leading citizens of his State. Like Edison, Andersen had a childhood full of uncertainty and difficulty. As a boy of nine he suffered from both polio and spinal meningitis, a combination that might have killed him, or at best, left him crippled for life. Fortunately Andersen overcame the effects of both of these killer diseases through unconquerable desire and gallant determination.

Still, trouble was just beginning for Elmer Andersen. Within five years, both his parents died, leaving fourteen year old Elmer and his siblings, two brothers and a sister, facing the prospect of being assigned to foster homes.

Determined to stay together as a family, the children managed by themselves to maintain their home in Muskegon, Michigan. Elmer found work as a newsboy. Here he learned that he had to fight in order to survive. The strongest of the paperboys controlled the best corners to peddle their papers and fought to keep them. The weapon of choice in these disputes was the knotted shoulder strap of the bag that contained the papers. Andersen says that he lost his share of fights, but applied the same tenacity selling candy on trains and household products door to door. He also managed to find summer work at the E.H. Sheldon company where furniture was manufactured for schools and laboratories. There he worked long hours for twenty-five cents an hour.

As soon as Andersen graduated from high school, he asked Mr. Sheldon for a job in sales, but was turned down because of a lack of experience. He was only seventeen. Undismayed, he enrolled in Muskegon Junior College and tried his hand at selling real estate while attending classes. Two years later he was back in Mr. Sheldon's office with the same request. This time the desire, determination, and potential of the young man must have been evident, because Mr. Sheldon gave him his chance as a regional sales representative in Minneapolis.

Desire is the fuel that drives us to the achievement of our goals. Vision is the ability to delay short-term gratification and see beyond the immediate present to a brighter future. In 1928, at a time when very few people went back to school after entering the work force, Andersen enrolled in the University of Minnesota's School of Business Administration.

In 1934, he heard of an opening with a little Minnesota company that was to change his life. H.B. Fuller Company, which specialized in the manufacture of adhesives, was looking for an advertising manager. Company revenues were small, but Elmer did his research and decided it had growth potential. It needed sales and marketing expertise, and he knew he could provide both. With enthusiasm he approached H.B. Fuller and got the job. By 1937 he was Sales Manager for the company. When owner Harvey Fuller decided to retire in 1941, it was thirty two year old Elmer Andersen who bought H.B. Fuller and launched an expansion plan that would fulfill his desire to make this small Minnesota manufacturer a Fortune 500 company. Andersen says, *"I never had a doubt about becoming a Fortune 500 Company. I just tracked how fast we were growing compared to the Fortune 500 and saw to it that we were growing faster. It was just a matter of time until we joined their ranks. The year it happened was much less important to me than making it happen. We made a chart projecting our growth and, sure enough, we got there."*

Already a success in business, Elmer Andersen sought ways to help people more directly. This desire led him into Minnesota politics, first as a State Senator, then as Governor. His main contributions in these years were in the fields of education and civil rights. He remembers vividly one episode from the days when he was trying to secure the passage of a bill he had co-sponsored, the Fair Employment Act which banned discrimination in hiring on the basis of race. *"There was a bitter debate but finally after a long evening we got the bill passed. I'll never forget as we left the chamber, how a black sergeant-at-arms touched my arm and said, 'Senator, tonight you have made me a real man.' That still moves me. Just think of it! There were people then so deprived that they questioned their own humanity."*

Desire. Intense desire. It shines through the lives of people like Kristine Johnson and Thomas Edison and Elmer Andersen. It is also a beckoning flame to those who have the desire to become one of the Diamonds themselves and make a difference in the lives of others.

Faithful adherence to a personal code of values that provides honor and direction

"Real integrity stays in place whether the test is adversity or prosperity".
-Charles Swindoll-

There is one luminous quality that lies at the heart of all Diamonds. It is the mystical and invisible element in human affairs known as integrity.

What exactly is integrity? Is it a sense of honor? Is it the capacity to distinguish right from wrong, and the determination when a choice is involved always to choose the right? Is it a kind of moral yardstick that some people seem able to apply while others don't? All these definitions are partially true. But integrity is greater than the sum of these parts.

DIAMONDS

One thing about integrity is certain: we all know it when we see it in action. Some time ago in Miami, Florida, an armored car loaded with cash rolled over in a freak accident, spilling literally millions of dollars in coins and paper currency into one of the poorest sections of the city. To residents it must have seemed like a gift from heaven as they saw $10, $20, and $100 bills blowing past their front doors. The temptation for those people to keep the money was enormous, and many gave in to it. But later that afternoon, a young mother with two small children appeared at the local police station with $19.98 that her children had found. She explained that although she had only the meager income from a minimum wage job, she wanted to teach her children a lesson in honesty. No rationalizations about finders-keepers. No justifications about the armored car's insurance covering the loss. Just the clear recognition that a person of integrity does not steal someone else's property. Remarkable? Yes. But it was integrity in action.

In one way or another, we all face this kind of challenge often during our lifetime. Suppose you make a dent in the car next to you in the parking lot? No one saw your mistake. Do you leave a note giving your name and address? Or do you just drive away?

Suppose your wife has lost a bracelet and you collect insurance. Then weeks later the missing jewelry turns up under a cushion in your living room sofa. Do you keep the money, or do you send it back? No one will know that the lost object has been found. But your conscience will know, and you will have chipped a splinter off your own integrity if you ignore it.

INTEGRITY

One definition of integrity is wholeness. Like an integer, a number in mathematics that is not divided into fractions, a people of integrity are not divided against themselves. They don't think one thing and say another, so it is virtually impossible for them to lie. People of integrity don't believe in one thing and do another, so they are not in conflict with their own principles. It's the absence of inner warfare that gives people the extra energy and clarity of thought that makes achievement inevitable.

Years ago in Detroit there was a young newspaperman named Norman Beasley. Quite often he was sent to interview Henry Ford. He enjoyed these assignments because the inventor was eccentric enough to make colorful copy. The great industrialist took a liking to the young reporter and talked quite openly about a variety of topics.

One day the question of reincarnation came up, and Beasley was astonished to hear Ford say that he believed in it completely. Ford continued by naming historic figures he thought he might have been in his past lives. Beasley took careful notes because he realized that he had quite a scoop on his hands, one that would certainly make headlines and please his newspaper editor, maybe even putting him in line for a bonus or a raise. But he was also aware that the editor might react with some skepticism, so he asked Ford if he would be willing to initial each page of notes as a guarantee of veracity. Somewhat impatiently, Ford did so. But then Beasley hesitated.

"Mr. Ford," he said, "I'm not sure that publishing this story would be a good idea for you or your company. It might lead some of your competitors to question your judgment—to their advantage. If I were you, sir, I think I would just tear this story up." And he handed back the initialed notes.

Ford looked at him with his shrewd blue eyes. "Perhaps you're right," he said at last. "I'll follow your advice. And I might add, I think you'll go far in this world. You're quite a remarkable young man."

Beasley did go on to a successful career in the newspaper world. Why? Because he was capable of putting integrity ahead of self-interest—and Ford knew it.

Building integrity into an organization is one of the most difficult challenges any executive ever undertakes. Why is establishing the habit of integrity, telling the truth, and doing the right thing throughout a company so hard? How can it be achieved with consistency and courage? How does an executive reach out to employees and maintain the integrity of the organization?

Bill George, Chairman and CEO of Medtronic, Inc., is a master at applying the glue of integrity to this hugely successful company. George has a warm smile and moves with an athletic stride that belies his fifty-six years. In January 1998, George was named in Business Week as one of the Top 25 Managers in 1997. The Top 25 came from a variety of countries and industries. Jack Welch of General Electric, Wendelin Wiedeking of Porsche, Sandy Weill of Travelers, Nobuhiko Kawamoto of Honda were among the 25 similarly honored. While the Top 25 are a diverse lot, they shared the common characteristic of being able to break from the pack and clearly out-perform.

George came to Medtronic as President in 1989 after eleven successful years at Honeywell. He became CEO of Medtronic in 1991. Between 1994 and fiscal year ending April 1998, revenues grew from $1.4 billion to $2.6 billion. Sales of $5 billion are projected for Medtronic in fiscal 2000, due to its series of acquisitions in calendar 1998. The year witnessed Medtronic becoming Minnesota's most valuable company in terms of market capitalization (shares outstanding, multiplied by stock price). Toward the end of the year its capitalization was $33.5 billion.

As a leader for the twenty-first century, George is a man with very clear ideas about what is necessary for corporate success in times of rapid change. He firmly believes that all of us have an inherent need to be making meaningful contributions to others through our work, and that this need lies at the heart of personal motivation.

Over and over, George emphasizes the need for leadership to be aware of values. *The latest focus in our organization is to stress leading by values. We believe that if all of us, employees and managers alike, agree on the values that guide our work, employees can be fully empowered to realize them.*

George has a strong conviction that for employees to be successful at Medtronic, they must be able to embrace the values of the company totally. Without published, constantly emphasized guidelines, the people of an organization cannot be expected to perform consistently.

When people speak of the "culture" of a company, what does that mean? It means the basic elements that make up a company's character, its values, its vision, its philosophy, its view of its own role in the society it serves. Sometimes this culture is confused, uncertain. Sometimes it is as clear and resonant as the ringing of a mighty bell. It all depends on the leadership that exists within the company itself.

In December, 1998, Medtronic again was named to *Fortune* magazine's list of the 100 Best Companies to Work for in America. Medtronic has an exceptional culture and is acknowledged both nationally and globally to be one of the truly great business ventures of our time.

Integrity at Medtronic is not optional. Bill George has instituted the Medtronic Compliance Program to ensure that all Medtronic associates understand the *"legal, moral, and ethical standards of conduct for all Medtronic employees."* It is a carefully worded document requiring review and an annual commitment in writing by everyone in the company. Department managers conduct educational sessions with employees to study and discuss Medtronic policies and how they apply to each person's daily work. By requiring an annual review and recommitment each year, the Compliance Program reminds every Medtronic employee that *"Medtronic's commitment to honesty and integrity is integral to its corporate culture."*

A special challenge for Bill George is the fact that cultures vary around the world and a company doing business in 127 countries might be expected to develop a different set of standards for those different countries. George and the compliance committee at Medtronic have put that notion to rest. *"All employees of Medtronic and its subsidiaries worldwide must adhere to Medtronic's policies—without exception.*

Medtronic's values and conduct must be generally consistent throughout the world while recognizing the cultural diversity of our global presence." Another challenge is how to deal with violations of policy or failure to live up to the standards of integrity outlined in the Medtronic Compliance Program. *"Employees must understand that violating Medtronic's policies will not be tolerated and may result in termination of employment if the violation exposes Medtronic to severe risk resulting from intentional wrongdoing or willful neglect. Less severe situations will result in immediate disciplinary action."*

The real challenge of maintaining integrity in an organization comes when someone fails to live up to the standards set in the compliance program. Bill George recalls ruefully a smart, ambitious Medtronic manager he personally promoted to President of an overseas operation. Although the executive said, in writing, that he practiced Medtronic's values, he had approved "promotional funds" that found their way into the foreign bank account of an important customer. Exasperated, he told George that if he would "just let us do business" in accordance with their standards, "we'll be fine." George countered, *"It's about Medtronic's values"*, and fired him. Where integrity is concerned, values cannot be compromised.

More and more it is becoming evident that it is impossible to be a whole human being without this shining attribute of integrity. True leaders recognize the difficulty of earning the trust of others without it.

DIAMONDS

Consider, for example, the track record of Lee Kopp, founder and president of Kopp Investment Advisors. Starting in June, 1990 he has built one of the top money-management firms in the country based on the principles of honesty, discipline, hard work, outstanding performance and philanthropy. Many people talk about such principles, but the people at Kopp Investment Advisors actually live them. For instance, one of the unique things about Kopp is that the company sets aside 10% of all earnings each year earmarked for a company foundation. This foundation has grown to the point where it generates over one million dollars annually that is given back to the community in scholarships, aid to abused children, and other worthy endeavors.

The company's reputation for integrity has been a huge factor in its success. Many individuals and institutions choose Kopp when they could select anyone in the world to look after their money. And their confidence has been rewarded in an extraordinary way. At the end of '98 those who invested in this Minneapolis-based money-management firm when it was founded in 1990 have seen a cumulative growth in their investments of 26.6% per year. Starting in 1990 with $20 million in client portfolios, the company now has over $2.5 billion under management. The first people who entrusted their money to Kopp in June of 1990 saw their investments grow by 101% in the first year alone. An investment of $100,000 in 1990 was worth $744,000 at the end of December 1998. It is estimated that there are 35,000 money-management firms in the United States, and only 10% ever break the $100 million mark. Kopp did it in eighteen months.

How does a company create such a vivid culture of integrity and outstanding performance in such a short time? How does it leapfrog into being one of the top money-management firms in just eight and a half years with a client base willing to invest a minimum of a million dollars for the opportunity to do business with it? Lee Kopp believes that *"You need to be there for your people. You need to lead by example. You need to provide integrity and a strong work ethic. If you work with a group of people where the level of expectations and standards are higher than most, you tend to move to that higher level, or at least to a higher level than you would otherwise."*

Given his company's record since inception in 1990, it would be easy for Lee Kopp and his associates to grow arrogant. But they haven't. When asked in an interview how he manages to keep his perspective, Kopp recalled an anecdote he had read in Fortune magazine. "A celebrity forced to wait in line turned to his wife angrily and said, 'If they realized who I am, they wouldn't treat me like this!' Her answer with a smile was, 'Do you know who you are? You're the son of a plumber who got lucky.'"

Kopp's choice of this story is not surprising. Like so many Diamonds, he has never forgotten who he is or what his roots are. His father managed a parking lot in downtown Minneapolis, earning $35 per week. Lee was the oldest of four children and had to help out. The lot also had a gas pump, and sometimes Kopp would hear businessmen discussing their investments as he filled their cars with gas. *"I soaked up everything like a sponge."*

DIAMONDS

As a boy, he did a tremendous amount of reading. His favorite books were biographies and autobiographies. From the stories of men like Theodore Roosevelt and Andrew Carnegie, he learned that you could move forward in life through your own efforts. According to Kopp, *"You could do it yourself."* Kopp learned at an early age that developing integrity requires the discipline of a proper mental diet, the habit of thinking positive thoughts, and reading the stories of men and women who have made an uncommon contribution to society.

Lee has been in the investment business for thirty-nine years and says that these last few years (in the small to mid cap stocks) have been the *"most difficult"* since the 74-75 stock market. In 1997 Kopp & Associates witnessed great volatility in their portfolios, exclusive of their new mutual fund, started in October 1997. They saw an 18% dip in the first four months, then a 55% increase in the May-September period, followed by a decline for the rest of '97 that left them minus .02 for the year.

In '98 Kopp Investment Advisors finished the year with their 4th quarter up a resounding 42%. This was a record quarter for Kopp. Yet the year as a whole was up only two percent. Their new mutual fund was down just less than 20% in the fifteen months since it started. Prior to the record 4th quarter Lee Kopp said, *"opportunities are incredibly attractive,"* and he was right.

Lee Kopp is a positive, upbeat person, well able to discuss both the up and down times in the cyclical investment business. He says, *"We are interested in the more volatile part of the investment business in the small and mid cap area"*. Consistency in how Kopp does business is very important to Lee. He says, *"you don't want to be something you are not."* For Lee and the people in their company this means staying true to their culture during the ups and downs of their business.

"One of the most important keys to maintaining integrity in any successful organization," Kopp says, *"is to hire only people who are capable of performing at a level consistent with the standards and values of the company."* Kopp puts it this way, *"The culture is critical. It is something we have established and it is not about to be affected significantly by any one individual. We don't need to hire a genius. We have enough good people on board already. However, one new disruptive person could negatively impact our organization, and I would not be comfortable with that."* In other words, Diamonds know that part of the integrity of leadership is to hire with integrity and to lead the culture in a way that guarantees consistency.

Diamonds have a genuine concern for the welfare and happiness of others. Esperanza Guerrero Anderson is the founder, president and CEO of Milestone Growth Fund, Inc., an investment company whose mission is *"to help minority people accumulate wealth."*

Esperanza packs enormous vitality and energy into her five-foot, one-inch frame. She is a warm lady with a big heart and strong convictions who speaks with passion about the things she values most.

Esperanza Anderson is a living example of a businesswoman of integrity dedicated to acting consistently within her beliefs and values. She is a person who has faced real adversity but has overcome that adversity to become a respected and trusted member of the American business community. Her company is based on the belief that if people are given the opportunity and guidance to succeed in business, they in turn will help others to prosper as well. She is committed to helping others develop their companies.

Esperanza was raised in Managua, Nicaragua. Her parents separated soon after she was born, so her mother became self-sufficient by selling real estate and renting part of their home for additional income. Anderson grew up with a keen appreciation for education and strong religious beliefs. Her education includes an undergraduate degree in business from Catholic University in Nicaragua, and graduate school studies in the United States.

Anderson believes that when minorities create wealth through owning their own businesses, they are better able to help their own communities. She is also well aware of the low self-image many minorities grow up with and the prejudices they experience when seeking financial help for a new business. *"I immersed myself in what it means to be a minority in America,"* she says. *"I was from another culture and didn't get the negative messages that handicap many minorities who are born here. I don't care if anyone thinks that I am a second-class citizen; I know that I am not. But if I had been born in this culture and had heard only that minorities are lazy, or are on drugs, or are criminals, my attitude might have been quite different!"*

Today Anderson is married, has three stepchildren, and provides a home for her eighty eight year-old mother and her ninety five year-old uncle in the Minneapolis suburb of Golden Valley. She describes herself as a former privileged Nicaraguan government employee whose background includes several years' experience as an administrator for the Central Bank of Nicaragua. She says she developed a social conscience when a revolution in her homeland forced her to sleep on the floor for two months to avoid stray Sandinista bullets. When she began to see her friends being harassed, arrested, and jailed for their anti-Communist views, she knew it was time to leave. She received a paid leave of absence from the bank, and planned one year in the United States to further her education. Six months into her sabbatical, her paychecks from Managua stopped abruptly. The Sandinistas had taken control, which left Esperanza with nothing, no job, no house or possessions, and no savings. She didn't even have the comfort of knowing whether or not her native country would welcome her back when and if she decided to return. *"I always thought I would go back, but I had been told that anybody who didn't embrace the new socialist-communist ideology would have trouble."* Instead, with the help of one of her college professors, she networked her way into a position as an international lending agent with First Bank Systems in Minneapolis, now part of U.S. Bank, with responsibility for five Latin-American countries. After three years of constant traveling, she yearned to become part of a community. However, this proved to be an excellent learning opportunity for Anderson, and provided her with the experiences necessary to form her own business in venture capital.

In her native country of Nicaragua, Anderson's name, Esperanza, means "hope", and hope is what she brings to those of minority backgrounds who would like to become American entrepreneurs. Since 1990, the Milestone Fund founded by Esperanza has provided money in the form of loans, or as equity, to minority business ventures that other financial institutions would consider too risky to finance. The fund has helped restaurant entrepreneurs, sheet metal fabricators, auto dealers, and construction contractors, among others. It is Anderson's responsibility to make good investment decisions so that money loaned is repaid with interest. This isn't always easy. When asked what she feels deeply about, Esperanza replies, *"I am paid to make sure that Milestone remains a long term player, which is my top priority. We play with our hands on the table. I want to be so whole and consistent that my behavior, image, talk, thoughts, and feelings are congruent. My values are honesty, respect, openness, and an ability to deliver what I promise."*

The Milestone Fund of $7.2 million is small compared to others in the field, but Milestone is the only one in the metropolitan area specializing in minority owned businesses. Anderson takes a very personal interest in her clients and makes herself available to them for counsel as well as capital. She also understands that success in business is one way of becoming part of the American mainstream. Anderson is using a powerful anti-discrimination tool, money, to help close the gap between people of different races. She puts it this way, *"Once you have proven that you can succeed financially in business, it's like everyone forgets about what your color or race may be."*

Anderson knows the importance of each investment

decision she makes, not only to her company and the client, but also to the minority community. Selecting the applicants most likely to succeed requires very good judgment. As she says. *"You don't invest in ideas. You invest in the person who can move the idea to reality."*

Through her work Esperanza Guerrero Anderson is making a difference in living her beliefs with the integrity so characteristic of Diamonds. *"My goal is to see a lot of minorities become wealthy, sit on the boards of big corporations and have a say in the social agenda. And not because they are part of the problem, but because they have the resources, experience, and the leadership to solve the problems."*

Winston Churchill once said, "Without courage, all other virtues lose their meaning." That can be said of integrity as well.

ATTITUDE

A positive state of mind that results in a can-do philosophy.

"Attitudes are more important than facts."
-Karl Menninger, M.D.-

These six words above, written by one of America's great psychiatrists, sound simple, don't they? Actually they contain the key to success in life—and also the key to failure. This is because in every area of living, attitude spells the difference.

When people meet with misfortune, for example, they react in many ways. A few years ago a relief worker in one of the flooded areas of the Midwest turned in this report. *"Often,"* he wrote, *"I go down a street where there are twenty houses, all of them afflicted with severe flood damage. But the outlook of the residents varies enormously. Some are filled with bitterness and disbelief. But there are also some who remain optimistic, who accept their problems with the determination to rise above them. You can tell right away which ones have the comeback capacity. Attitudes make all the difference."*

The Diamonds of this world know instinctively that this is true. That is why they remain constantly aware of their own attitudes, trying to adjust them, trying to improve them, trying to understand them.

Michael Jordan, the charismatic, professional basketball player for the Chicago Bulls retired in 1999. He is a walking illustration of the words: winning attitude. Even in the heat of competition there is often a smile of enjoyment on his face. In the history of basketball he is the best there has ever been at his job.

In the final game of the 1998 NBA finals, he gave a never-to-be-forgotten performance. He scored 45 points and his passing and defense were at their usual high standards. With 18.9 seconds left in the game and the Bulls down by one point, Jordan stole the ball from Utah star Karl Malone. Dribbling down the court and sizing up the situation, Jordan saw Bryon Russell, who was guarding him, lose his balance. Seizing the opportunity, Jordan took a shot at the point of the circle. Fans all over the world watched the flight of the ball on its way to the net. Michael's jump shot connected with 5.2 seconds left and the crowd exploded.

Jordan said, *"When I got the ball, my thoughts were very positive. I saw that moment and the opportunity to take advantage of it. I never doubted myself."*

Jordan, the ultimate go-to guy, had not only led his

team to the 1998 NBA title, but also won his sixth Most Valuable Player Award in the playoffs, a feat never before accomplished.

Can you imagine how many twelve-year old boys watching that game were thinking, "If only one day I could be like Michael Jordan." Of course they would have to begin by growing to the considerable height of six and one-half feet tall. But young, aspiring Michael Jordans would be wise to note that he prepared thoroughly, worked hard, and believed he could be the best. It is his attitude that nurtured his talent, and made him the widely acclaimed winner in his work that he truly has been.

Regardless of what we do for a living, regardless of our goals and aspirations, regardless of our age or position in life, it is the degree to which we take control of our attitude that determines our destiny.

Another key attitude that often shines out in the careers of Diamonds is commitment.

Years ago in New York City there was a young Italian immigrant named Bernard Castro who could barely speak English. Hoping to overcome this handicap, he enrolled in a remedial night class being offered at a school on the other side of town, at least two miles away. There were more than two hundred other students in the class.

One cold winter night, a blinding snowstorm swept into the city. By the time the young man started to walk to his class, the storm had reached blizzard proportions. He had no overcoat and his shoes were thin and needed repair but he forced himself to keep going. When at last he reached the school, he found it closed. A custodian who answered his knock said, "Are you crazy" No one's going to come out on a night like this. Go home."

Discouraged and disappointed, the young man turned back. But as he trudged along, a sudden thought came to him. Of the over two hundred people in his class, he was the only one who had cared enough to make the effort. He was the only one that night who was truly committed to his education. And this knowledge, he said years later, stayed with him through all kinds of setbacks and disappointments. That same level of commitment enabled Bernard Castro to build a highly successful furniture company.

One of the most difficult challenges faced by many of us is the comfort zone we slide into when we have succeeded in a career. What once was fun and challenging has become routine and boring. The more comfortable we become, the more resistant we are to change and the more difficult it is to recapture the once positive attitude that brought us success. Many of us are afraid that by changing our lives we will have to give up the luxuries and privileges that we worked so hard to achieve. We also have to face that lingering doubt, "Am I prepared for the possibility of failure that accompanies a career change?"

A good example of a man who has learned to follow his heart and his head is Tom Holloran. Tom has chosen four careers. He is a man who not only enjoys a challenge, but also, when he knows the time is right, can move on and accept new challenges.

Tom is a purposeful individual, a little on the stocky side, whose twinkling eyes reflect a keen sense of humor. A natural leader, he invariably becomes the Chairman of the many boards and committees with which he is involved. This is because the people who work with Tom can see his obvious integrity and self-assurance and are willing to trust him completely.

Tom readily learns the skills and vocabulary that go with each new job. Because of his positive attitude and adaptability to change, he makes the transition seem easy. He was first tested as a young naval officer during the Korean War aboard a destroyer. There he had to negotiate for practically all of the basic necessities required by his shipmates, from garbage removal to a daily water supply.

Tom started his first career as a practicing attorney and as his former law partner John Byron relates, "He became famous for his rolling stone lunches." He would invite one person to lunch and on the way would add four or five others. He was constantly building a lifelong network of contacts. When Tom decided it was time to leave the law firm and become a businessman, his many friends cut across all racial, political and religious lines.

In 1967 Tom Holloran joined Medtronic as executive vice-president. One of the questions of the day was whether or not Medtronic was to become a global company. Although the company lacked the people and the money, they knew that a global presence was necessary because they were finding demand for their products to be worldwide. Setting up an independent distribution network was important if Medtronic was to grow internationally at a faster rate. When asked if his legal background made him the one best suited for the task, Tom replied, *"I had no expertise whatsoever, but there wasn't anybody else to do it."* He accepted the challenge of extensive travel to Europe and South America. In 1968 one-third of Medtronic's business came from overseas, and the foundation for a world-wide company was being established.

The excellent chemistry between Tom and Earl Bakken, the co-founder of Medtronic, was a huge asset during this critical time. Tom says, with a laugh, that part of that chemistry was because, *"We didn't know what we were doing. We were brainstorming, looking for ideas, and it was intoxicating."*

In 1973 Tom became President of Medtronic. As he continued over the next few years, he found that Medtronic was becoming more of his identity than he wished. Tom says, *"The issues of the company followed me all of my waking hours."* In 1975, after much soul searching, he knew that it was time to tell Earl Bakken that he was leaving the company they had worked so hard together to build. Earl took this news graciously, with great warmth and understanding. He told us that he couldn't have built Medtronic without Tom Holloran. Today Tom Holloran continues as a valued director of the Medtronic Board.

It was time to move on. Tom did not have a job when he left Medtronic, nor did he have an inkling of where his next stop would be. However, in less than six months he was in his new role as Chairman and CEO of Inter Regional Financial Group, Inc. Today it is Dain Rauscher, one of the leading financial service companies in the Twin Cities with annual revenues over $800 million. Again, Tom had to learn a whole new language and adapt to an entirely different set of products. This time investments that could help people become financially independent and companies grow became his new passion. Tom was like a racehorse on a new track. Dick McFarland who succeeded Tom as CEO, and is currently Vice-Chairman of Dain Rauscher says of Tom: "He is universally trusted."

Tom's leadership and positive attitude remain invaluable to him in his fourth career. Today he is a professor at the University of St. Thomas Graduate School of Business. He has learned from each of his careers and tells each of his classes at St. Thomas that he has three expectations of them:

> First, he expects his graduates to be professionally competent.
> Second, he expects them to be caring people.
> Third, he expects them to contribute to the community.

When asked about any failures along the way and what he learned from them, Tom quickly replied, *"Sure, in the early eighties I relied too heavily on the integrity of a manager."* This resulted in improper reporting of financial information, which Tom says cost IFG over one hundred million dollars. In his words, *"It was a searing event."* The leasing unit involved was closed, three hundred jobs were lost, and as Tom relates this story you sense his disappointment over the loss of those jobs that he feels to this day. When asked what he learned during that turbulent time, Tom replied dryly, *"I became more alert to early warning signals."*

How does a Tom Holloran develop the confident attitude to start over in new careers not once but four times? Tom says without hesitation that his parents deserve much of the credit. *"They raised me in a cocoon of positive attitudes, always encouraging me to try new things and giving me the support I needed to do well in all of them. They planted in me the feeling that I could succeed in almost anything. They taught me that meeting challenges was fun and success in one area would lead to success in another."*

There was nothing mysterious or magical about the way Tom's parents brought him up. They spent time with him, reading to him, talking to him, sharing interesting dinner-table conversations with him. When possible, they took Tom with them on trips, exposing him to different backgrounds and different cultures. *"I'm not sure what or who I would be today,"* Tom says, *"if I had had a less loving childhood."*

Diamonds often have benefited tremendously from positive upbringings and a history of successes built upon successes. They have not allowed themselves to be spoiled by success or to fall into a comfort zone. They have learned that a positive attitude can be sustained through new challenges, curiosity and a willing adaptability to change. This attitude has permeated Tom Holloran's entire professional life. He has renewed himself each ten or twelve years through accepting new challenges that have been personally fulfilling for him.

ATTITUDE

Another key attitude that often shines in the careers of Diamonds is perseverance. When Chuck Denny came to Magnetic Controls (later named ADC Telecommunications) as its new President and CEO in 1970, sales totaled about six million dollars. Less than a month after he assumed his new position their bank abruptly canceled their line of credit. The books had been improperly stated, and a surprise loss of about one million dollars faced the new President. Imagine how painful this was for Denny who had moved his family back from Europe, where he was employed, in order to take the reins of what he thought was a promising company. This was no place for a defeatist. Denny immediately made the difficult decision to lay off just over one-third of the work force, a reduction of two hundred thirty-two workers.

Denny's commitment did not go unnoticed or unrewarded. Charles Bell, the former Chairman of General Mills, who owned close to 50% of the company, made the move to guarantee the ADC debt. Chuck Denny later called this a *"gesture of nobility."* This act of loyalty and support for the new CEO made a lasting impression that is evident today in Denny's tone and manner as he tells the story of the days when ADC was at the brink.

Although others would say that it was Denny's strength of character that saved the day, he sees it somewhat differently. When asked about the major obstacle that he faced in the early days, Chuck reflected a few moments and said, *"Myself."* He had come from a large company culture where sometimes *"the quality of the excuse was more important than the quality of the result."* As the CEO of a much smaller ADC, there were daily cash flow challenges and no doubt as to where the accountability for results resided.

A key development in turning the company around was the growth of IBM as a customer. *"ADC would not have been able to achieve the success it has without the support of IBM as a customer,"* Denny says today. *"Working for IBM was like working for a master teacher."* Designers and others in the manufacturing sector at IBM went out of their way to help, and they shared information about the manufacturing standards that worked for them. *"It was a true partnership,"* says Denny, illustrating once again how, when a group of people are totally committed to success, unexpected allies and circumstances come to their aid.

Chuck Denny and his team had won major battles, but not the war. Their willingness to rise to the occasion and overcome adversity was to be challenged again in the summer of 1989 when a Wall Street investment firm made an unfriendly overture to ADC and purchased 4.9% of their stock. ADC executives requested that they cease purchase of any more stock, because exceeding 5% would require public disclosure. This could put the stock "into play," which is a term referring to rampant speculation that can lead to a takeover or buyout.

Denny was determined to *"resist to the end."* He was by then a seasoned executive who understood something about character and courage. He rejected advice to pay a premium to the investment firm for their holdings to make the aggressor go away. Instead he made it clear that he would not capitulate. *"My position is that I'll die before I'll do that."* The Wall Street executives got the message. In early 1990, their shares were sold (at a handsome profit) and the threat to ADC's autonomy as an organization was over. Denny's courage of his convictions had made a big difference.

One of the most delicate tasks for any CEO is choosing his successor. Here again, Chuck Denny displayed the kind of perseverance that has marked his brilliant ADC career. In 1988, after three years of having another executive in the COO position, Denny decided it was not the right fit for all concerned and took back the COO position until he could find the right person. He had envisioned his successor in place by then because, as Chuck said, *"I had hoped to be moving into other aspects of my life by now ... something beyond business."*

It wasn't until 1990 that Chuck named William Cadogan as President and Chief Operating Officer of ADC. With sixteen years experience at American Telephone & Telegraph Co., Cadogan had the technical background that Chuck was seeking.

Denny said he hoped to leave the CEO post within two years, and this time it happened. On November 1, 1991, William Cadogan was named Chief Executive Officer of ADC and the mantle had been passed. Cadogan's performance since being named CEO has been outstanding with sales increasing from $200 million in 1991 to over $1.38 billion in 1998. In a recent conversation, Denny lauded William Cadogan as the single greatest stroke of good fortune that the company has had in decades and praised the former COO for hiring him.

Chuck Denny is a rare person in many ways. Without the benefit of technical experience, he rose to the leadership of a growth company in a technical industry and, with a creative, persevering attitude, overcame many obstacles. In so doing he built an excellent company and took the necessary steps to leave the company in the hands of a very talented successor.

———————

Another key attitude common to many Diamonds is a passion for excellence. They seek it in their co-workers and they demand it of themselves. If you ask them why this is so, they will tell you that their hunger for excellence grows out of the fact that they love their work. They are convinced that their work has meaning and, based on that belief, an attitude of excellence emerges.

Nina M. Archabal is the tremendously capable and energetic Director of the Minnesota Historical Society, the largest state historical society in the country with its 15,206 members. In September of 1997 she was one of ten individuals to receive the first annual National Humanities medal from President Clinton. The award recognizes individuals whose work has deepened the nation's understanding and engagement in the humanities. A petite dark-haired woman, Nina lives an attitude of excellence. She typifies the quality of the work done by her organization in serving others as well as possible. In 1992 Nina Archabal led a quest that resulted in the opening of a magnificent new 427,000 square foot

Minnesota History Center. It inaugurated a new era of service to the people of Minnesota and visitors from across the nation.

During the previous decade, trustees and staff had shared a guiding vision, "We have envisioned a place that draws the public in, fires its imagination, and responds to its hunger for an understanding of the past. We have envisioned a building alive with people from morning until far into the evening...families in the museum; scholars, genealogists, and teachers in the reading rooms; children absorbed in a variety of things, from dramatic presentations to craft activities; crowds arriving for classes, lectures, films, symposia and plays; and school and tour buses lining the entrance drive...a vital cultural and educational center with something going on all the time."

When asked about her commitment to excellence, she says with a smile, *"Joy of the work is what drives me. Whatever I do has to be done as well as I can do it."* She goes on to say, *"School children are the most important clients we have."* Nina adds that the children go away from the Minnesota History Center today with a feeling that they, too, are part of that history.

Nina's enthusiasm for excellence is contagious. Ken Rothschild served as President of the Board throughout the History Center building project. He recalled that Nina told them in the beginning, *"I'm going to get together the people that can do the building right. I need to find the best people possible."* She proceeded to do that. Ken goes on to say that in addition to hiring very competent people, Nina had the ability to take people in her own organization and give them an environment in which they could take chances, expand their horizons and grow. "She can create an excitement that is compelling."

In talking to Nina about people who helped her, she smiles when she mentions one of her special people, Rachel Tooker. While Rachel was finishing her studies for a Master's Degree, she was a volunteer at two of the society's historic sites, as well as a paid tour guide. Everything she touched carried the stamp of excellence. Nina found herself drawn to the person and her capabilities. Shortly after Rachel earned her degree Nina hired her. During the first week on the job, and having assessed the size of the project, Rachel walked into Nina's office and announced "Nina, forget your plans for the weekend—we'll need to work both days and nights." Nina said, *"I hired Rachel hoping she would give me a hand. Instead she took me in hand."* Ken Rothschild recalled that Nina liked hiring people who had strong views. If they didn't agree with her, she wanted them to tell her. In the environment she created, they did. When construction ended in January 1992, the Society could report that their massive building project was coming in on time, within budget and without litigation.

The message that Nina communicates to everyone around her is a simple one: Love your work and let that love be one of the catalysts in determining your attitudes.

————————

Diamonds are aware that the words they use every day significantly affect their own personalities. As Dr. Maxwell Maltz says in his book, *Psychocybernetics*,

ATTITUDE

"What we say and do is stored in our subconscious mind and becomes a part of us."

Knowing this, it is wise to deliberately avoid using certain words and consciously replace them with others. Take a word like *"frustrating"* for example. When people proclaim that they are frustrated, what are they really saying? Isn't it that they are baffled, thwarted, upset, blocked from reaching the goal or accomplishing their objective? Instead of yielding to this negative word, why not choose another one: *"challenging."* In so doing, mood and outlook are changed in a positive way. Verbal habits such as this have a definite impact on our attitudes.

Down through the ages an interest in words and skill in using them has been one of the hallmarks of Diamonds. Abraham Lincoln is a clear example. His Gettysburg Address remains one of the classics of literature. And yet, knowing Lincoln's background, one wonders how such genius ever came to light. One can only conclude that the lives of Diamonds are not limited by the circumstances of birth. There are attitudes that can overcome a rocky upbringing, however deprived.

What was the attitude in Lincoln's case? Surely it was a hunger for learning. Lincoln's mother was a young girl named Nancy Hanks who could not write, and perhaps never went to school. When she was twenty-two she married a man who was illiterate. Tom Lincoln was described by neighbors as "a rover, a ne'er-do-well, floats about from one place to another taking any kind of job when hunger drives him to it."

Business affairs were beyond Tom Lincoln and he soon realized that he belonged to the woods. He purchased a farm on a vast stretch of treeless land known as the "barrens." In winter it was bitterly cold. On a Sunday morning in 1809, Abraham Lincoln was born in this desolate place amidst a howling February storm, with blowing snow finding its way through the cracks in the log cabin.

In 1816 Tom Lincoln moved his family into the dense forests of Indiana. It was early winter when they arrived, and Tom built a structure where the fourth side was wide open to the elements. Their food consisted primarily of wild game and nuts. It was a difficult early childhood for Abraham Lincoln.

At the age of fifteen Abe knew his alphabet. Yet he could not write, and could barely read. Then in the fall of 1824, a backwoodsman called Azel Dorsey came into his life. Azel began teaching in an old cabin. Abe and his sister would walk four miles each way through the woods in order to go to class. Reading assignments were chapters from the Bible. During that time, Abe took a fancy to the handwriting of Washington and Jefferson. In fact, he became so good at copying their styles that his neighbors would walk many miles just to have him write their letters for them. Out of this slender education, Abe developed a thirst and hunger for learning. He wrote essays that attracted notice, yet his formal schooling totaled only twelve months. In 1847 he went to Congress. While filling out a biographical form, he came to the question, "What has been your education?" To which Abe replied, *"Defective."*

Years later, after being nominated for the Presidency,

he said: *"When I came of age, I did not know much. Still somehow, I could read, write and cipher to the rule of three, but that was all. I have not been to school since."*

How did this beloved President overcome such a start? For Abe, reading was the way. It was his passion for two and a half decades. He read and reread the Bible, Aesop's Fables, Robinson Crusoe, Pilgrim's Progress, and Sinbad the Sailor, all possessions of his stepmother. He borrowed books from everywhere. For the first time, he read the Declaration of Independence and the Constitution of the United States.

Learning was constantly on his mind. He would walk fifteen miles to hear lawyers argue in the river towns. He imitated the Sunday preachers in Little Pigeon Creek Church. His companion while working in the fields was a joke book called "Quinn's Jests." It was from these beginnings that Lincoln went on to become perhaps the most respected President in United States history, and it was his learning attitude that made the big difference.

"Attitudes are more important than facts." These words of Dr. Karl Menninger, quoted at the beginning of this chapter, are profoundly true. And it is also true that one of the greatest of human freedoms is man's ability to choose his attitudes, regardless of circumstances. In the pages you have just read, such choices were made, as follows:

Michael Jordan chose being a winner.

Bernard Castro chose commitment to his work.

Tom Holloran chose self-renewal through new
   challenges.

Chuck Denny chose perseverance.

DIAMONDS

Nina Archabal chose the pursuit of excellence.
Abraham Lincoln chose a hunger for learning.
They *chose an attitude* and it changed their lives. Can you say the same?

MISSION

A sense of dedicated, focused purpose.

*"Mission is an image of a desired state of affairs that
inspires action, determines behavior,
and fuels motivation"*
-Charles Swindoll-

In one of his poems, Longfellow speaks of leaving
"footprints on the sands of time". These footprints are
rarely discernable at first in the meaningful careers of men
and women. They become visible only after years of dedicated effort, usually focused on a single worthwhile goal.
But when those footsteps are firmly implanted, almost
always some significant aspect of living has been changed
for many people.

Go back some eighty seven years to the small southern

city of Savannah, Georgia. It is March 1912, and a middle-aged, childless widow recently returned from England has picked up the telephone and is calling her best friend, a local schoolteacher. *"Nina,"* she says, *"I want you to come over here right away. I have something for the girls of this city and of this country and of the whole world, and we're going to start it tonight!"*

What Juliette Low had was a concept that she had learned in England from her friend Sir Robert Baden-Powell, the founder of the Boy Scouts. Juliette Low could see no reason why the same principles and ideals should not be applied to girls as well as boys. She had no experience in organizing anything; she was handicapped by a severe hearing loss, her family smiled indulgently at her enthusiasm. But before many weeks had passed she had organized two troops of Girl Guides, as they were called then, in her hometown. When she died fifteen years later, thanks to her persistence and dedication there were hundreds all over the nation. Today there are more than three million Girl Scouts and their numbers keep growing every year.

Or consider the set of footprints left in England by a dedicated social worker named Cecily Saunders. Soon after the war ended in 1945, her work brought her into contact with a young Polish immigrant who lay dying in a London hospital with no family or friends. He spoke to her of the isolation and loneliness that he felt, and she in turn told him of a dream she had of a Home or Shelter where people like him could spend their last days in dignity, surrounded by caring people. When he died, the young Pole left her five hundred pounds 'to be a window in your Home.' She went on to study medicine, but she never relinquished her dream. In 1965 construction was started on a 70-bed building. The cost eventually was close to half a million pounds, all of it donated. In this building Cecily Saunders achieved her goal, which was to make people and the medical profession realize that death isn't just the surrender of life, but a positive act worth doing well, an act that people need help in accomplishing.

Today the Hospice concept has spread all over the world. Every year thousands of terminally ill patients and their families are helped immeasurably by the vision Cecily Saunders had so many years ago. The footprints she laid down are still there for others to follow. This is because the footprints that Longfellow described more than a century ago are not just static marks in the sands of time. They are a path, a guide, and a goal-pointing blueprint that others can recognize and follow because the goal itself is so worthwhile.

There is one key characteristic that people like Juliette Low and Cecily Saunders have in common. It is not just the ability to dream. It is something more than a transitory vision. It is a profound sense of mission; a conviction that it is their duty and their obligation to cling to their image of a desired state of affairs until the image becomes reality.

Sometimes the word mission itself seems to run like a shining thread through the lives of such people. More than two hundred years ago, a Franciscan friar named

DIAMONDS

Junipero Serra volunteered to leave Spain and go to the rugged coast of California with the goal of bringing Christianity to the scattered and primitive Indian tribes that lived there. His plan was to create a series of missions (the term comes from the Latin word missa, which in English means *sent*), that would be strung out over more than six hundred miles from the place where San Diego now stands, to a point north of San Francisco. In the next few decades, against all manner of hardships and setbacks, Father Serra and his colleagues carried out this astonishing dream. Eventually there were twenty-one of these missions spaced about a day's journey apart, leaving "footprints" that are still highly visible today.

What tenacity of purposes it must have taken! Hostile Indians, sometimes pirates, political intrigues, days of scorching heat and bone-chilling wind and rain. It is said that Father Serra traveled more than six thousand miles on foot or by muleback in pursuit of his dream, planting new missions, building up some that had been destroyed, baptizing thousands of natives. Perhaps nowhere else in the New World had a sense of mission seen such spectacular results.

Diamonds have always known that every one of us needs a strong sense of purpose if we are to be motivated to bring about positive change in others and ourselves. And there can be nothing fuzzy or unclear about this sense of mission. It needs to be carefully defined, preferably in writing. There are countless cases where carefully crafted written Mission Statements have resulted in incredible success.

An outstanding example is the Mission Statement that has guided the Medtronic organization for the last 39 years without the change of a single word. All of the employees at Medtronic are familiar with and constantly reminded of the company's Mission Statement that is the foundation for priorities, plans and work assignments.

Back in 1960 when co-founder Earl Bakken wrote Medtronic's Mission Statement, he could not have imagined the impact his foresight would have on the organization. The Mission of Medtronic is printed on a card provided to every Medtronic employee. When Earl Bakken was still active at Medtronic, he talked about the mission like an evangelist. *"It gives purpose to our work, describes the values we live by, and is the motivation behind every action we take."*

The Medtronic Mission Statement:

* To contribute to human welfare by application of biomedical engineering in the research, design manufacture, and sale of instruments or appliances that alleviate pain, restore health, and extend life.

* To direct our growth in the areas of biomedical engineering where we display maximum strength and ability to gather people and facilities that tend to augment these areas; to continuously build on these areas through education and knowledge assimilation; to avoid participation in areas where we cannot make unique and worthy contributions.

* To strive without reserve for the greatest possible reliability and quality in our products; to be the unsurpassed standard of comparison and to be recognized as a company of dedication, integrity, and service.

* To make a fair profit on current operations to meet our obligations, sustain our growth, and reach our goals.

* To recognize the personal worth of employees by providing an employment framework that allows personal satisfaction in work accomplished, security, advancement, opportunity, and means to share in the company's success.
* To maintain good citizenship as a company.

The company remains totally committed to "restoring lives through medical innovation" and its mission is a subject of constant communication throughout the organization.

In November 1989, the Minnesota Center for Corporate Responsibility sponsored a workshop designed to help others better understand both the origin and the impact of Medtronic's Mission Statement. Co-founder Earl Bakken stated, *"We wrote that first Mission Statement, and we said that this is really what we want to do with the rest of our lives, dedicate them to restoring people."*

"Medtronic's mission is not just words on paper," says Medtronic executive Kristine Johnson, *"it's constantly communicated and reinforced."* According to CEO Bill George, *"It's not a creed that you just accept. You have to be passionate about it."* It is especially critical that both the mission and values of Medtronic be constantly repeated and made visual, as Medtronic grows worldwide. As Bill George explains, *"The culture of an organization is made up of values and norms. Medtronic employees in Japan and Minnesota may have different cultural norms, but their business principles can be guided by the same set of values, if they all know the company's mission"*.

His thinking about the importance of purpose for employees is well illustrated by a talk he gave at a breakfast meeting attended by some large investors. As

George said later, *"I started out the breakfast meeting by saying, 'the purpose of Medtronic is not to maximize shareholder values.' I saw some puzzled looks. Then I said, 'the only reason for us to be in business is to maximize value to patients.' Fortunately, I got a few smiles and a few nods out of that. I think we have to ask ourselves what is our purpose for being? At Medtronic we feel very passionately and very fervently that we are in business to maximize the value to patients."* He went on to say that Medtronic's real bottom line was restoring 1.3 million people to full life and health in a twelve-month period. *"That is what we are proudest of."* At Medtronic the mission is alive and well.

At one time founder Earl Bakken met with every new employee to explain the Medtronic Mission and to present each with a special medallion. The medallion bears a symbol of a patient rising from a gurney following surgery, a man restored to health. Earl asked the medallion recipients to put it on their desks at work, as a reminder that they are there to fulfill Medtronic's mission.

It is not enough to write a powerful Mission Statement and then mount it on the wall. The purpose of the organization has to be constantly reinforced in ways that cannot be forgotten. There must be a passion for the Mission that is nurtured and never allowed to die.

The best way to give the mission life and keep it burning is sharing with your people the impact on customers. Each year at Christmas time, Medtronic celebrates the holiday with a special program attended by fifteen hundred employees in the atrium auditorium at Medtronic, and by many additional employees via video conferencing. Six patients and their physicians are invited to tell their stories illustrating how the use of Medtronic products has changed their lives. This is the most special day of the year for many Medtronic employees. Earl Bakken, author of the mission and company co-founder, never misses the event.

Bill George tells how the Medtronic Mission came to life for him at the company's holiday program in 1989. Shortly after George had joined Medtronic, a decision had been made to spin off a division manufacturing drug pumps that had lost over $25 million in a ten-year period. By the time of the holiday party in December, no buyers had been found. Earl Bakken suggested to George that he take a look at a young man named T.J. Flack, age eighteen, who was coming to the party with his doctor. Flack had been a victim of spastic cerebral palsy since birth. In addition to the debilitating effects of the disease, he experienced surgery annually for thirteen years. The surgery gave him some relief for a while, but in less than a year the spasticity would return. Finally he had had enough, and refused any additional surgery. George relates that, *"At age eighteen, T.J. Flack became one of the first patients in an experimental program at Pittsburgh Children's Hospital to receive the Medtronic Implantable Synchro Med Drug Pump with the drug baclofen. As a result his health improved dramatically to the point where six years later he was graduating from college and playing wheelchair basketball."*

Medtronic also kept making drug pumps and as Bill George tells it, *"T.J. Flack's experience served to illustrate how in business you can be too focused on the bottom line. When a new venture gets close to death, you can shut it down, or spin it off at just the time when it is going to take off."* Now George says that drug pumps are the fastest growing line in the company.

T. J.'s story at the annual holiday program is just one example of how the Mission Statement is kept alive at Medtronic. Medtronic employees know, and are constantly reminded, that a Mission Statement is not just words on paper; it is the very purpose for the organization's existence and brings focus to every Medtronic employee's life.

Important as a written Mission Statement is concerning one's work, it is even more significant when a person has a passion for writing their own personal mission statement summarizing the meaning and purpose of their life. If the statement includes goals, ambitions, and plans for helping others, so much the better.

It's a long way from the red clay roads of rural Georgia to the corporate offices of General Mills in Minnesota, a long, long way. But that is exactly the journey that has been traveled by a special woman named Reatha Clark King. Reatha's story is the tale of one woman's desire for education, a desire that led from poverty and illiteracy in rural Georgia to a sense of personal mission of enhancing and providing education for self and others.

Today Reatha Clark King is the President and Director of the General Mills Foundation, a foundation that dispenses over $16 million per year. A strikingly attractive woman, she looks every bit the Homecoming Queen she once was. It is easy to forget that this genuinely engaging woman holds board positions on a number of the largest and most influential institutions in the Midwest.

Reatha's accomplishments would be extraordinary for anyone, but are all the more impressive in the context of what she had to overcome along the way. As a young child she learned what a limited education could mean in life as she watched her father, an illiterate farm hand, and her mother with a third grade education struggle to make ends meet. Reatha's mother, Ola Mae Clark, separated from her husband in 1945. She headed north in search of better work and higher pay. This left Reatha and her sisters to live with their widowed grandmother, Mamie Watts, who was also illiterate. Says Reatha, *"From this experience I learned first-hand about the problems that illiteracy causes people."*

Ola Mae, Reatha's mother, had to travel far and often in search of better work, a point not lost on Reatha. *"I can see that my mother, as a single parent, had to move around a lot to pursue a good job and better housing. Neither of these things were readily accessible to an uneducated woman."* Reatha and her sisters did what they could to help out, working at odd jobs during their years at Moultrie High School, including maid service in private homes, painting broom handles, picking cotton, and gathering tobacco. *"More and more I wanted to get an education so that I could get better work and have more options than my parents,"* says King. *"My objective was to overcome poverty."* Even then, Reatha knew that she had a secret weapon, which was confidence in her own ability. The mission of personal education, born of necessity, would be with her for the rest of her life.

Lack of money was also a driving force, especially during her college years at Clark College in Atlanta.

Although she worked part time in the registrar's office for thirty-five cents per hour, she often was unable to pay tuition in time to take the semester exams. *"Lack of money is the most painful memory of my undergraduate years. Paying for books, tuition, room and board, and miscellaneous expenses was difficult, even with a $250 tuition scholarship and a job,"* says Reatha. *"My mother was earning eighteen dollars per week at the time with two daughters in college."* She came away with a new appreciation for the value of financial aid and the kind of stress experienced by students who lack funds.

Twenty year old Reatha Clark King graduated *summa cum laude* from Clark College with a Woodrow Wilson Fellowship and enrolled at the University of Chicago to begin work on a doctorate program in Chemistry. Because of her fellowship, she no longer had to worry about educational expenses. *"I left Clark College in June of 1958 with a stronger sense of my values, a keen sense of what's right and wrong in relating to people and, above all, a feeling for what black people could contribute to this country if given the opportunity to do so."*

After graduating from the University of Chicago, Reatha Clark King went on to an assistant professorship at York College, a part of City University of New York. The young woman with a personal mission for education was now an educator, sharing the lessons she had learned in a big city environment far from the cotton fields of Georgia. There was spirited debate and significant tension on the campus during Reatha's time at York. Feelings ran high over the Vietnam War. Faculty was split as to whether the permanent home of City University should be in an inner city or suburban location, and there was significant racial tension. Says Reatha about this period of her life, *"Even though I was a new kid on the block, I was not neutral about any of these issues, nor was I ambivalent about my preferences. I wanted the permanent campus to be placed in the inner city neighborhood of Jamaica, Queens. Knowing what the presence of higher education could do for a community, I felt that placing the campus there was the best solution."*

By 1970 the administration had noticed Reatha's leadership ability and she was named Associate Dean of the Division of Natural Sciences and Mathematics. Under her direction, the division established academic computer services and new degree programs in biology, chemistry, geology, physics, mathematics, medical technology, occupational therapy, and environmental health science. Four years later, in 1974, Reatha saw her dream for York College in Jamaica, Queens become a reality as a new building was constructed in the inner city that became a symbol to the community of York's commitment.

By this time, the question in Reatha's mind was whether she should return to industry or pursue a career in higher education. She decided to continue her education by seeking a master's degree in business administration at Columbia University. When she returned to school in 1974, however, she was pursuing her mission from a new perspective. *"I was studying for the sheer joy of learning."* Reatha Clark King had discovered that the desire for learning that had been the secret of her rise from poverty was also a means of self-fulfillment and personal pleasure for her.

In 1977 King found the career opportunity that would

allow her to pursue her personal mission for education using all of her talents as a leader, educator, and community servant when she was named President of Metropolitan State University in Minnesota. Reatha saw the need for a creative, unconventional institution sensitive to the needs of working adults seeking additional skills, knowledge, and a degree to compete for better jobs. *"Metro State did not have the conventional symbols of a university, such as a campus with dormitories and basketball teams. The University was a real fishbowl with absolutely no separation between 'town and gown'. From the beginning, I viewed Metro State as a unique setting where I could make a special contribution. Without the frills and symbols of higher education, we could focus solely on the needs of our students and communities."* Under her leadership, Metro State flourished, growing from an average enrollment of 1,600 students in 1987 to 5,000, ten years later.

Since 1988 Dr. Reatha Clark King pursues a new mission as President and Executive Director of the General Mills Foundation. She is known internationally as a pioneer in social change, and is respected as a leader in the fields of education, business, and philanthropy. In recognition of her contributions, she has received twelve honorary doctorate degrees.

In many ways, Reatha's personal philosophy reaches out to touch everyone who comes into contact with her. *"How do you defuse anxiety in your life? Keep your personal framework of values clear and clean. Why is it important to understand other people and other cultures? Because the world is getting smaller, and such understanding is essential to peace. Don't worry too much about language barriers. A smile is a universal means of communication. And remember, when you're trying to understand other people, they are trying to understand you too."*

Optimism is at the core of Reatha's beliefs. *"Don't worry about limitations or things you haven't got. Identify with what you have and build on that. Don't shy away from new challenges. Enjoy the moment, wherever you are. Just keep going, and finally you'll reach a state in life where you begin living to serve others. That's what it's all about."*

Donna Shalala, President of Hunter College, sums up Reatha Clark King very nicely: "People like Reatha Clark King should be cloned for the good of the nation. Everything she puts her hand to succeeds. She combines wisdom with energy, strength with compassion, foresight with commitment."

In other words, Reatha is one of the Diamonds — and a splendid one.

In her book *Pathfinders*, Gail Sheehy writes, "My research offers impressive evidence that we feel better when we attempt to make our world better ... to have a purpose beyond one's self lends to existence a meaning and direction."

One of the real Pathfinders by Sheehy's definition is Gladys Brooks, a woman who for over fifty years has led the way in breaking through the glass ceiling that has unfairly held so many women back in business and public life. She has been determined to break through these barriers all her life. Gladys Brooks looks like everyone's favorite grandmother yet she is a formidable lady; direct in speech and full of gumption. It is easy to see how this charming lady has influenced so many people over the years. Her sense of personal mission was brought to life by her father who told her at a young age that, "You can do just as well as a man." Gladys Brooks never forgot that comment as she became a role model for others and assumed leadership in helping women of her generation break down the barriers.

Gladys recalls that at the age of eleven, she was asked what she wanted to do when she grew up. Her reply was that of someone who had already found her mission in life. *"I want to walk in the front door of the Minneapolis Club."* This conversation took place in the 1920's when women were not allowed membership in prestigious clubs, and were treated as second class citizens when access was permitted. *"Those things rankled me,"* she said.

Brooks has proven in her lifetime that much can be accomplished by someone who not only sees inequities but also is determined to do something about them. Cynthia Threlkeld, head of the Minnesota International Center, says of Gladys, "She is a catalyst. She's an incredible woman. She's a natural networker, helping you get connected. Everybody who knows her, adores her."

Her sense of personal mission as a leader in the movement for fair treatment of women came naturally to her, even though she was far ahead of her time. She has a fine sense of history and a family heritage of citizenship. According to Brooks, *"My mother was an early suffragette, marching to Washington, and she was active in the peace movement during World War I."*

One of the things that has made Gladys Brooks so special is that she is not thought of as a partisan politician, but as a consensus builder. She has led as a role model, doing what needed to be done and refusing to accept no for an answer when something violated her sense of right and wrong. According to friends, "Brooks' strength has been her knowledge of the community, her personality, and her dedication." Her other great strength has been the sense of personal mission that she has carried with her since the age of eleven when she first understood that there was a need for a new sense of place for women in America.

Gladys has been a pathfinder and role model in many ways. In 1987 she was honored by the American Society for Public Administration for a lifetime of achievement in public service. Gladys was the first woman to run for Mayor of the city of Minneapolis as the candidate of a major party. During the sixties she headed the Governor's Commission on Human Rights, and found herself in the Deep South fighting for the rights of men and women who were imprisoned for their efforts to help minorities. She served tirelessly as the only woman on the Minneapolis City Council, and took a leadership role in encouraging other women to seek elected office.

Today bright young women are emerging from college, confident that they can carve out careers for themselves in business, politics or any other profession without worrying unduly about gender discrimination or glass ceilings. They feel free to pursue their goals in life, to follow their dreams. The tremendous strides women have made toward equality are due in large part to women like Gladys Brooks—real Diamonds who have dedicated their time, energy and unswerving personal mission to make that freedom happen, to make those dreams come true.

Being Receptive to Fresh Ideas, Methods and Challenges

"Man's mind, stretched to a new idea never goes back to its original dimensions."
-Oliver Wendell Holmes-

If there is one rule of living that is honored by Diamonds everywhere it is this: Learn and grow. They believe that regardless of age, regardless of circumstances, a person has an obligation to keep expanding in the four key areas—**mental, emotional, physical** and **spiritual**—that are the cornerstones of human personality.

Diamonds know too that the growth process should be on a broad scale. To advance in only one area and neglect the others results in an uneven performance like an automobile with tires that are out of balance. What makes such progress achievable is the quality of open-mindedness.

How, for example, do you add the growth dimension to your **mental** development? One way is to review and up-date your goal-setting capacity. Being open to setting and accomplishing goals takes much of the mystery out of success.

Each of us needs goals in our lives to provide inspiration, purpose, and focus. The challenge is to have balanced goals so that they contribute to a balanced lifestyle. Everyone needs family and personal goals, business and career goals, finance and self-improvement goals. Setting balanced goals eliminates the habit of living aimlessly.

Brian Tracy, the well-known authority on personal effectiveness and human achievement, calls the ability to set goals with action plans for their achievement "The Master Skill". To be effective, goal setting requires an awareness of certain principles.

-Your goals must be consistent with your values.
-Your goals should be achievable, but they should also expand your mind.
-Your goals must be written. The very act of putting your goal on paper provides clarity and focus.
-Your goals must be specific and measurable.
-Above all, summon up your self-discipline, because this is the key to Earl Nightingale's definition of success as "the progressive realization of a worthy ideal".

Goal setting should be a lifelong pursuit at any age. Some years ago when Dr. Norman Vincent Peale, the famous New York minister, was in his ninety second year, he was honored by his alma mater, Ohio Wesleyan. Seated on the stage, a bit weary after giving a talk to the student body, Dr. Peale let his eyes close.

OPENNESS

Apparently he had drifted off in sleep, but when a member of the audience called out, "Dr. Peale, what goals are you having these days?"—the minister opened one eye and said promptly, *"Short-term or long-term?"* The audience exploded in delighted laughter, but Dr. Peale was not merely being humorous. He was reminding us that goal setting should be a part of living as long as life lasts.

Goals can be both tangible and intangible. Tangible goals are represented by income, house, car, boat and similar material objectives. A few of the intangible goals are a healthy self-concept, warm relationships and self-determination. Most of us would settle for a healthy balance of tangible and intangible goals in living our own unique lives.

There is one remarkable technique that is highly effective in expanding all four areas of human personality: mental, emotional, physical and spiritual. That special technique is known as *"affirmation"*. In affirmation a goal is stated as a positive present-time fact. For example, let's say that you have the goal of becoming an excellent sales person. You then construct a simple affirmation such as 'I am an excellent sales person'. When this affirmation is given daily repetition, it soaks into your subconscious mind more easily, and has a better chance of becoming active in your life.

Affirmations are always done in the present tense. Use of the present tense is accepted and recorded by your subconscious mind as a present-time fact. If you use the word 'will', as in "I will be an excellent sales person", then the subconscious mind records it as a future event.

Norman Vincent Peale was a strong believer in the tremendous power of affirmation as an aid to goal setting. He was certain that, if used consistently, it could change and enhance lives—including his own. He was always trying to improve the wording of his affirmations. Early one morning in London, more than a dozen years ago, he picked up a piece of hotel stationery and wrote down the following:

An Affirmation
I affirm that God's power is rising in me,
Renewing and healing my body,
Giving power to my mind.
Giving me success in my work.
I affirm health, energy, enthusiasm, and the joy of life.
All this I owe to Jesus Christ, my Lord and Savior.
He has given me the victory principle for which I
thank Him every day.

There can be little doubt that Dr. Peale's boundless energy and creativity were based on the convictions expressed in those eight lines. The *'joy of life'* that he mentions, spilled over in many directions. When young people sought him out with doubts about their futures or their careers, he would say to them, *"Shoot for the moon. Even if you miss it, you'll land among the stars!"* To members of his congregation, who seemed timid or uncertain, he would recommend the classic affirmation of St. Paul: *I can do all things through Christ who strengthens me.* *"Just ten words,"* Norman would tell them, *"but if you say them aloud as you begin every day—and believe them—they will change your life."*

In the late 1950's John and Helen Boyle originated a four-day seminar, first called Executive Dynamics and later renamed Omega. After personally attending this course in the early sixties, Major General Sam Phillips had a special session conducted for key people in the Apollo program. The importance of self-concept was a relatively new idea at the time and was the major theme of the course. *"I like myself unconditionally"* was the Master Affirmation taught. Today some simply use *'I like myself'* or *'I like myself whole-heartedly'*. It is up to the individual. There is a freedom in liking yourself, and prizing your own uniqueness.

It was recommended that a person practice the Master Affirmation either in the first half-hour upon arising in the morning or during the last half-hour before going to bed. The rate at which the subconscious mind receives and accepts an affirmation is accelerated as we come out of or go into sleep. The affirmations are done sitting in a relaxed and comfortable position in a chair, keeping the legs slightly apart, with feet on the floor and hands resting palms up on the knees.

A twenty-three second affirmation technique was taught. A person reads their affirmation, which takes about three seconds. Then with eyes closed for ten seconds, the desired outcome is visualized. Then for ten seconds the feeling of the desired outcome is remembered and held. Let's take a teacher for example. The affirmation, *'I like myself whole-heartedly'* is read. For ten seconds the teacher visualizes a recent experience where a former student told the teacher what a difference the teacher has made in their life. For another ten seconds the teacher remembers the gratification experienced on hearing the student say that. For those who have difficulty visualizing there is the option of reading and repeating, aloud if possible, the Master Affirmation five times with feeling, so that it registers more strongly in your subconscious mind.

Here is a simple practice that we call the *Diamonds' Minute*. Within ten minutes of arising, seat yourself in a chair and say two things:
First, 'I like myself whole-heartedly'.
Second, select your most important goal at this particular time in your life. Then construct an affirmation in the present tense around this goal.

Repeating both of these affirmations with as much feeling as you can generate takes less than a minute and is a valuable way to etch these goals indelibly into your subconscious mind. Affirmations are catalysts that enable you to reach your goals more quickly when you think and believe. The key is consistently continuing the practice

Another effective way to use the affirmation idea is in your personal mission statement. By crafting your purpose for living in the present tense, and reviewing it at the beginning of each day, you are cultivating a priceless habit. More and more individuals are realizing the impact of a personal mission statement on careers, marriages, friendships and many other aspects of living. The reward of writing your personal mission statement is often a marvelous sense of clarified purpose. You state why you are here on this earth and what you believe your purpose is. Most of us have never done this. Many of us have written specific goals, but writing a personal mission statement is new.

Sometimes it helps to ignite the process by having an affirmation or two as a framework on which to build. Your first sentence simply says what you believe your personal mission is. The second sentence could be something like "So that I accomplish my personal mission statement ever more effectively I like myself whole-heartedly." You have introduced the Master Affirmation as the second sentence of your personal mission statement. If you wish you can stop right there. By reading or memorizing and repeating those two sentences every day, you have given birth to your personal mission statement. What you are doing is making a statement with the purpose of your life.

For those wishing to go further there are no limits. Your personal mission statement is your property. You are the sole architect. Further expansion of your personal mission statement can come from the eight words that gave us our acronym for Diamonds: Desire, Integrity, Attitude, Mission, Openness, New-mindedness, Decisiveness and Service.

Start perhaps by using only two or three of them. You will find that constructing your personal mission statement is a mental game that gives additional energy and purpose to your life.

Parents, pre-school and elementary school teachers have become increasingly knowledgeable about the importance of a strong self-concept for the healthy **emotional** life of small children and the impact it

69

has on effective performance in school and adult life.

A great pioneer in education was the noted educator Maria Montessori. The first woman in Italy to receive her M.D. degree, Madame Montessori was a ceaseless experimenter, observer and dreamer. In her experimental work with *"defective"* children, she developed a series of educational methods that proved astounding in their results, with the *"defective"* children out-performing the *"normal"* ones on state examinations. From these methods she developed a system for general education and promoted it throughout the world. At the heart of these methods was Montessori's conviction that children learn best when given a balance of freedom and guidance in an environment where the children can make choices.

Montessori taught that the first six years of a child's life is an age where parents and teachers help prepare the skills of the child, so that the child can feel the power to act successfully on its own. Letting children do as much as they can for themselves fosters early independence and self-confidence. However, Montessori warned, *"To let the child do as he or she likes, when the child has not yet developed any powers of control, is to betray the idea of freedom. Real freedom instead is a consequence of development, the construction of the personality reached by effort and one's own experience."*

From ages six to twelve comes the discovery of a child's social self. The world opens up to the child and they begin asking some deep questions. Wise is the parent or teacher who takes the time to answer these questions, and feels they are important. This is the conscious learning phase that starts with imaging power and unlocks the key to the imagination. This is a time of working in groups and collaborative learning. Central to a good Montessori class is *"concentrated work"*, which teaches the child the joy of losing one's self in their work. This is a powerful agent for independence and self-confidence.

The years of twelve to eighteen are the adolescent years of self-discovery. Children are emerging from their elementary school years and are rebuilding themselves in relation to others, while needing the support of their peers to nurture their growth. As a Montessori child, Anne Frank, the well- known victim of the Nazis in World War II, said, "Parents can only give good advice or put them on the paths, but the final forming of a person's character lies in their own hands."

Today in the United States there are approximately two hundred American Montessori International schools that follow the principles that Montessori laid down. One such school is the Lake Country School located in south Minneapolis, and founded in 1976 by Larry and Pat Schaefer for children in pre-school through eighth grade. Their goal was to create an authentic Montessori School which, when organized properly, could blossom into a model along the lines Maria Montessori intended. Lake Country's Mission Statement is clear. "Lake Country School is an urban-based Montessori community whose purpose is to help children prepare themselves for life. We respect differences and strive to mirror the rich diversity of our world. We foster independence, critical thinking, and respect and responsibility to self, to others and the earth."

A few years ago the heads of two leading private schools in the Twin Cities, Frank Magusin of St. Paul Academy-Summit School and Ty Tingley of The Blake School in Minneapolis, and now at Phillips Exeter Academy in New Hampshire, praised the graduates of Lake Country, stressing how well they performed in their high schools.

Maria Montessori wrote, *"the basic job of the educator is to aid life, leaving it free to unfold itself"*. Kathleen Coskran, the current head of Lake Country School says, "that is what we are about at Lake Country; being present in the lives of children who are deeply engaged in the wondrous task of self-discovery and self-construction."

Kathleen says that the "prepared environment" is key. The children must have materials that are right for their age, and they must be properly organized. Great significance is placed on the relationship of the teacher to the child. How well they know each other is important. "The teacher makes a commitment to the child. It can't be over at five o'clock."

When Pat Schaeffer is asked about her thoughts she says, *"Since Montessori education strikes at the heart of human development, struggles can emerge in its process. In a world ever rushed by limits of time and plagued by frayed nerves, good communication with the children and between the adults can become a frequent challenge. Parents and teachers can lose their sense of trust and shy away from taking the proper time to communicate. When patience and time are invested in the process of communication, a community builds up around the children. When adults fail to make that investment, struggles ensue, and the process of human development is impaired."*

Pat and Larry Schaefer talk of openness as being extremely important in a child's development. Pat says, *"The child comes into this world with an open mind. We hand the culture to the child. How to do that without closing the child's mind is the trick. It is the interest of the child that drives the learning process."* Much of what is done at Lake Country promotes what is necessary for this to take place.

It is important for students to make choices and develop themselves. In pre-school at Children's House for example, there is a button-shirt frame and a presentation on how to do it. The child has the freedom of choice either to learn this skill or not. Self-confidence comes from doing it, and learning takes place.

The Schaefers also believe that the student needs a strong emotional network of support. The friendships children make and how they treat one another play a key role here. They are encouraged to practice friendliness and to think of themselves as kind, for kindness can be leadership. The idea of *I Like My Better Self* is stressed. The trust that parent and teacher have in one another and the staff getting along sends a message to the children. All of this creates a sense of community, and the upbeat atmosphere of Lake Country School, together with the children's enthusiasm for learning, reflects this.

Self-confidence is a major component in the Lake Country experience, and positive peer group experiences play an important role. Larry Schaefer provides some interesting experiences for the Lake Country Junior High students. One of these takes place during a four-day bike trip where they average 25 to 35 miles a day. All the students, regardless of their particular love of the sport, have to bike and are encouraged to support one another. There is strong staff support and encouragement of the students. Larry says, *"The phenomenon that always happens as the students meet and overcome the challenges is that they become elated by their successes and discover hidden powers and talents in themselves. Comments such as 'Wow, I didn't know I could do this!' 'I'm so proud of myself!' and 'I didn't walk a single hill!' are not uncommon."*

Every second year at the beginning of the school year, the Junior High students take a fifteen-day Odyssey trip to Crow Canyon Archaeological Center, New Cortez, Colorado. The trip is organized around certain challenging learning experiences. One of these is to climb Specimen Mountain in Rocky Mountain National Park. There is a 2,500 ft., three-hour climb to the 9,000 ft. summit. The students climb in three groups, one group having some climbing experience, but many in the other two having no experience at all. Everyone climbs as long as they are physically able. As they struggle up the mountain, a certain magic occurs and distracts them from their difficulties. The beauty of nature along the trail, the camaraderie of suffering together, the laughter and encouragement of their peers, lifts them up and before they realize it the climb is over. The self-discovery process continues.

Larry Schaefer feels there is a fundamental challenge

in the community experience of traveling together in harmony. Students not only learn the disciplines of camping such as the setup, cooking and cleanup, but more important, they learn to resolve conflicts and be a support for one another. Nine to ten nights of camping are involved. Over the years the staff at Lake Country has been rewarded by letters from campground owners, and the comments of people camping next to them. They say that they have never witnessed Junior High students so self-directed, cooperative and respectful of one another and those around them.

Lake Country School is an example of an environment that encourages independence and breeds self-confidence. It teaches students the importance of openness to new ideas and choices that are right for them.

At the same time it only makes good sense for a caring parent to monitor the learning environment for their girl or boy. No one school is right for everyone. To make changes when it fits and where possible can make a tremendous difference in the self-confidence and growth of a young person.

Throughout her career Maria Montessori had to face skepticism and sometimes harsh criticism from educators who simply could not see the merits of her new thinking. Their minds were closed to any innovations that did not fit their preconceived ideas. It took a woman with great strength of character to persist in spite of them.

———————

It is important to keep an openness about the **physical** aspect of your life too. In Canada Drs. Evan and

Wilfrid Shute pioneered the medical use of Vitamin E. The location of the Shute Institute was in London, Ontario, one hundred twenty-two miles north of Detroit. In 1933 Dr. Evan Shute, a recent graduate of the University of Toronto Medical School, began his work with Vitamin E.

Early in 1946 there was mounting evidence that clinical use of Vitamin E held some value for heart patients, and two cases were very close to home. Dr. Shute's mother could not walk across the kitchen without chest pain, so on February 15, 1946 she started taking Vitamin E. After just one week her condition had improved to the point where she could garden outdoors once again. Dr. Shute's barber, Roy Bickwell, had been in bed for a week with angina pain. Within three weeks of Vitamin E treatment Roy was not only back to work, but also was playing drums in a local musical group.

On November 5, 1948 inaugural ceremonies were held at the Shute Institute with approximately ninety people in attendance, and a new chapter on clinical Vitamin E treatment was launched at 10 Grand Avenue in London, Ontario. Consistent with the integrity of the man, Dr. Shute established the Shute Foundation on a non-profit basis in May 1947. This was done "in order to make clear to everyone that Dr. Evan Shute was observing the professional tradition that he should make no personal profit from the obvious financial advantages accruing to his discoveries." Throughout his working life at the Shute Institute, he was paid a salary only. In the twenty-six years that followed approximately forty thousand patients, including those from foreign countries, were treated for a variety of cardiovascular conditions, burns, and other physical ailments.

Through his clinical work Dr. Shute observed that Vitamin E has several functions in the body. First, in its role as an anti-oxidant, "E" stops the process of unprotected fatty acids in the body being destroyed, which contributes to cell aging. Secondly, Vitamin E opens up collateral channels to encourage blood circulation. In this way necessary nutrients and oxygen are carried safely throughout the body. Third, "E" prevents clotting, often the cause of strokes, and does it safely.

Starting in the late forties, if the medical establishment in the United States had been open enough to collaborate with the Shute Institute, many of our friends and family members would have led healthier and longer lives. As of 1974 no Shute papers on Vitamin E were permitted in the Journal of the American Medical Association, nor did the AMA send anyone to view the Shute Institute work in spite of many invitations to do so. The Shute Institute published their own journal, *The Summary*, and sent out twelve thousand copies throughout the world each year in an effort to keep people abreast of their clinical findings.

Finally, in 1992 at the American Heart Association meeting in New Orleans, two new major medical studies including one with women and one with men— reported that taking daily doses of Vitamin E appeared to cut the risk of heart disease by one-third to one-half.

In England, in March 1996, *Lancet* published the results of the Cambridge Heart Anti-oxidant Study, involving just over two thousand patients with severe heart disease. Just over half the patients were randomly selected to receive daily doses of Vitamin E in either the 400 or 800 IU dosage. The others were given an inert placebo. After seventeen months the Cambridge University researchers found that those taking Vitamin E had only a 25% risk of developing a heart attack as compared to those on the placebo.

The clinical evidence provided by the forty thousand patients of the Shute Institute over a twenty-six year period from 1948 to 1974 was close to overwhelming. One would think that the positive indications from these studies would have provided the stimulus for open minds in the United States medical community to try Vitamin E in collaboration with the Shute Institute rather than wait decades for another study. But this was not the case.

The medical profession does too many good things, and is too important to all of us not to be open to ideas from others that work for their patients. It is not just the medical profession. It is all of us in any type of work or personal situation, who face the challenge of staying open to ideas from others that work better than the ones we have now.

Why is having an open mind so difficult for most of us at different times in our lives? Often we say to ourselves, "I already know the answer to that" when, if we would just give the idea a fresh look, it might uncover an insight that works for us. Making a habit of learning with an open mind is not always easy, but it is a vital part of healthy growth as a person.

What about the **spiritual** dimension in human lives? Every year billions of dollars flow into research at various levels in the private and government sectors. Education and science are beneficiaries and correctly so. Yet how odd that those who research spirituality do so for years, and even a lifetime, with little recognition or money. One exception to this attitude of indifference is Sir John Templeton who addressed this disparity back in 1972 when he created the Templeton Prize for Progress in Religion. Mother Teresa was the first recipient in 1973. At the time she was not well known. Six years later she was awarded the Nobel Peace Prize, and by the time of her death in 1997, Mother Teresa was known the world over.

Meeting with Sir John Templeton at his office in Nassau, one is struck by his vigor. He is a remarkably youthful man, who just happens to be eighty-six years young. His favorite physical exercise when he is at home is to walk in the ocean for thirty-five minutes in water up to his neck. It works wonderfully well for him.

Sir John was born in 1912 in rural Winchester, Tennessee. He graduated from Yale in 1934 and became a Rhodes Scholar at Oxford. In 1937 he went to work on Wall Street. In 1940, at the age of twenty eight, he started his own fund management company, which by 1954 evolved into the Templeton Growth Fund. His companies eventually managed twenty two billion dollars in assets. In 1987 Queen Elizabeth knighted him for his philanthropic efforts. These include his endowment of Templeton College in Oxford and the College of Bahamas in Nassau. He retired from investment management in 1992 and devotes his time now to the Templeton Foundation. He has been involved in the writing of many books and has lived in Nassau since 1969.

DIAMONDS

Sir John Templeton feels strongly that the Nobel Prizes overlooked spirituality and its importance to the world. Therefore he established a foundation that funds the Templeton Prize in perpetuity at a level guaranteed to exceed the Nobel Prizes. Today at over a million dollars, it is the world's largest monetary prize awarded annually. *"The objective of the Templeton Prize is to stimulate the knowledge and love of God on the part of humankind everywhere"*. Exceptional originality in advancing the world's understanding of God is the goal of the prize. Templeton plays no part in selecting the winner. He does ask the international panel of nine judges to consider all religions. Buddhism, Christianity, Hinduism, Islam, and Jewish faiths have all been represented over the twenty-five years since its inception.

An interesting dimension to the Templeton Prize is the quality of the nine judges chosen each year to select a winner. Mrs. Anwar Sadat, widow of the former President of Egypt, Norman Vincent Peale, the legendary minister of Marble Collegiate Church in New York, Dr. Nagendra Singh, President of the International Court of Justice at the Hague, William Simon, former United States Secretary of the Treasury, Margaret Thatcher, former Prime Minister of Great Britain, Professor Sunite Kurmar Chatterii, who was National Professor of India in the Humanities and President of the Senate of Bengal, and Mr. Masakazu Echigo, Buddhist layman who was President of C. Itoh Co. in Japan are just a few of the diverse people who have served as judges for the Templeton Prize.

Early in our conversation, Sir John said, *"My hope would be to change people's minds so they would welcome new things in religion. I doubt any human being knows one per cent of God, so we should be humble. If we are more humble, we are more open and tolerant. If you're impressed with how little you know, you get enthusiastic about learning more. I don't see why I shouldn't welcome a missionary from the Buddhist faith whose heart is in his scriptures, and who wants to explain them to me".* Templeton, a Christian, once told another interviewer, *"I think it is only openness to listen carefully to the Buddhist missionary."* He added, *"Tolerance comes from humility and love".*

In 1995 the Templeton Prize winner was a mathematical physicist, Dr. Paul Davies, who adheres to no particular faith. This Australian scientist's inquiring mind has probed into the workings of the universe and helped breach the barrier between science and religion. He is known for his important contributions to theories concerning the nature of time, black holes, and the beginning of the universe. He is also regarded as a powerful source of knowledge for the big questions of modern physics. He has authored more than twenty books on these subjects. Dr. Davies contends that our ability to understand math and science and therefore know and calculate the physical universe "evidences purpose and design to human existence."

Spiritually, for each of us, there are options as we live each day. We can be open-minded and explore daily prayer, the Golden Rule, and countless other spiritual matters, or we can simply choose to close off the spiritual side of our lives.

Sir John Templeton chose to explore spiritual matters. For the past forty years it has literally been his personal mission in life. He is well known in his business career for asking someone to open his company's meetings with prayer. He says, *"I think all careers are more successful and satisfying if you use spiritual principles. I can't think of a single exception"*.

In his life Sir John Templeton has done and is doing much to advance the importance of spirituality in the lives of people throughout the world. The real question for the rest of us is am I open-minded and courageous enough to explore the spiritual aspects of my life that I cannot fully understand. History is full of Diamonds who gave an affirmative answer to that question.

––––––––––

Dr. George Washington Carver, born in 1864 of slave parents, won international fame for his work in agricultural research. Since his death in 1943, some eighteen schools have been named in his honor. He revolutionized the agriculture of the South by developing 350 products from peanuts alone and over 150 from the sweet potato. This allowed southern farmers new sources of income by growing crops other than cotton. Dr. David Fairchild of the U.S. Department of Agriculture said Dr. Carver possessed "one of the finest and most extraordinary minds I ever met."

Dr. Carver was a firm believer in prayer. When he discovered that the great spiritual principles in the Bible were basic laws of the universe, he acted on them. When asked what he acted on first, he replied, *"I took this verse in the Bible, 'In all thy ways acknowledge Him, and He will direct thy paths'. I found that it* worked. *This led me to explore more to discover the Infinite, and now every morning at four o'clock, I tune in to the Great Creator. Before I begin my work in the laboratory I pray to the Great Creator to help me, and then inventions come through as from an outside source."*

When someone wrote to Dr. Carver asking about prayer, he replied: *"My prayers seem to be more of an attitude than anything else. I indulge in very little lip service, but ask the Great Creator silently, daily and often many times a day, to permit me to speak to Him through the three great Kingdoms of the world which he has created—the animal, the mineral and vegetable Kingdoms—to understand their relations to each other, and our relations to them and to the Great Creator who made all of us. I ask him daily, and often momently, to give me wisdom, understanding, and bodily strength to do His Will; hence I am asking and receiving all the time."*

Abraham Lincoln, too, was a man who spent a lot of time in prayer. One of his friends once asked him how he could afford to waste, as he put it, so much time on his knees. Lincoln replied: *"I would be the greatest fool on earth, if I thought that I could sustain the demands of this high office without the help of a strength which is far greater than my own."*

Of the four great areas of living...mental, emotional, physical and spiritual, perhaps the spiritual is the most important. And the wisdom it contains is the reward for those who open their minds and hearts to this aspect of their lives.

In sum, as you come to the end of this chapter, close

the book and ask yourself some probing questions. Is there a consistent thread of openness running through all the major areas of my life? Do I welcome challenging ideas that tend to stretch my mind? Is a steady pattern of growth leading me into new dimensions of self-discovery? Am I growing in my capacity to treat all people with kindness, tolerance and love?

Don't be discouraged if you can't answer those questions with an unqualified 'yes'. If you can answer them with a hopeful and sincere 'I'm trying', that may be all the answer you need to give.

NEW-MINDEDNESS

**Exploring your imagination
for creative solutions.**

*" The significant problems of our times cannot be
solved by the same level of thinking
that created them"*
-Albert Einstein-

The chapter you have just read was a discussion of one of the most important qualities that Diamonds strive for: the quality of openness. This chapter deals with a quality equally important: the quality of new-mindedness.

There is a distinction that should be made here. In openness, a person is receptive to fresh ideas and concepts and proposals that other people have originated. They come from outside. In new-mindedness, one is capable of originating plans and strategies and solutions on one's own. Such ideas come from inside.

This quality of new-mindedness is absolutely essential when it comes to solving major problems of living. In fact, the more difficult the problem, the more important new-mindedness becomes.

Abraham Lincoln knew this well. The first months of the Civil War were dark times for the Union. Battles were being lost. Generals were proving themselves incompetent. There was gloom and defeatism at home.

In his second annual address to Congress, delivered on December 1, 1862, Lincoln faced up to these realities. It is easy to visualize him, tall and gaunt and somber, standing before the assembly of law-givers, willing to admit that things were going badly, but ready to offer a solution, if they would just listen to him. *"The dogmas of the quiet past,"* he warned them, *"are inadequate to the stormy present. <u>We must think anew and act anew</u>."*

New-mindedness, he was saying, would save the Union. Nothing else would. And eventually, with the Emancipation Proclamation and other innovations in strategy and weaponry, it did.

Today, new-minded thinking is the launching point for progressive companies. If you doubt that, consider the case of Medtronic and its co-founder, Earl Bakken.

Medtronic and some of its people weave in and out of the pages of this book because they have consistently created a culture from which all of us can learn. This culture continues to make a difference in the lives of people inside and outside the company. The people of Medtronic are a great example of what happens when people live and work in a contagious atmosphere of serving their fellow human beings. It is an organization that has applied technology dramatically to enhance the lives of people around the world. However, back in 1949 there was no Medtronic, no pacemaker industry, and people with heart conditions often were dying before their time. All of this changed because of one new-minded electrical engineer and entrepreneur, Earl Bakken.

Bakken grew up in northeast Minneapolis, Minnesota, in the 1920's. As a boy, he developed a fascination with electronics. His uncle, a professional electrician, was concerned about young Earl's playing with the open electric insulators that were common in those days. This uncle once told Earl's mother, "You've got to stop that boy from playing with those wires or he's going to electrocute himself." We can all be thankful that instead, Earl Bakken's mother encouraged her son's interest in electricity and supported his work with crystal sets and vacuum tubes. In so doing she nurtured the growth of a person who was to make a huge difference in the lives of many people.

Earl Bakken and his brother-in-law Palmer Hermundslie founded Medtronic in 1949 while Earl Bakken was in graduate school at the University of Minnesota. Earl had earned his undergraduate degree in electrical engineering and was in the habit of visiting the hospital at the University looking for a way to earn some money. Hospitals were just beginning to use sophisticated electronic equipment as a result of new technologies created in World War II. When this equipment required repairs, the hospital would send it to local radio repair shops. Bakken and his brother-in-law concluded that, *"Maybe there is a business in offering a good, competent, quality repair service in the field of medical electronics."* So the two set up shop in a neighborhood garage.

In 1954, Bakken had an experience that was to change his life and eventually make Medtronic a giant in a new industry. Bakken had become acquainted with the team of surgeons at the University of Minnesota headed by Dr. C. Walton Lillehei and with their research into human heart repairs. Many children were dying in the fifties because of a hole between the ventricles of the heart that caused inadequate blood flow and lack of oxygen in the body. Babies with this condition had a bluish tinge and were referred to as "blue babies."

Earl says, *"Dr. Lillehei wanted to open these hearts and sew a patch over the hole between the ventricles. To do that he needed to stop the baby's heart. When you stop the heart for any length of time, you have to have some way to keep the brain and the body oxygenated. In those days there were no mechanical oxygenators, so they connected the child to a parent with the same blood type and circulated the blood through the parent and then through the baby. In that way they could stop the baby's heart and yet keep the baby oxygenated with the parent acting as the oxygenator."*

There was potential for high mortality but fortunately results were good. They would stop the baby's heart, go in and sew a patch over the hole, close up and the baby would come out of surgery in quite good shape. With that repair the children generally could live normal lives."

However, not all the babies lived and Earl said, *"the obvious answer was to use a pacemaker to keep their hearts going. At that time the only pacemakers were large vacuum-tube machines. For power they had to be plugged on the alternating current wall plug line. Working with interns and residents, we developed a method of connecting a wire to the baby's heart at the time of surgery, bringing it out through the chest and connecting it to the wall-powered unit."*

The need at the time was to create a battery powered device that would eliminate the fear of power failures and provide greater portability than wall-mounted units. Again, Earl Bakken showed his ability as a new-minded thinker. He had run across a circuit for an electronic metronome in Popular Mechanics Magazine that was intended to improve the performance of pianists. Bakken concluded that the same principles would work in a battery-powered pacemaker, reasoning that the rhythm or pace of the heart is the same as that of the metronome. Four weeks after being asked by Dr. Lillehei to design a battery powered pacemaker, Bakken came up with the first device that was used on a child and it worked. The word quickly spread, and Medtronic was in the manufacturing business to stay. It wasn't until the decade of the sixties that Medtronic designed the first implantable pacemaker.

How was Earl Bakken able to make that leap in imagination that brought about the lifesaving pacemaker technology? In those days there was no such device that we would think of as a pacemaker today, and some felt that tampering with the operation of the human heart bordered on "playing God". According to the new-minded Bakken, his imagination was triggered by a movie that he watched back in 1931. The movie was Frankenstein, in which the evil doctor creates a monster with a gigantic jolt of electricity. Bakken says that one result of seeing that movie was that it helped create his life-long interest in the role electricity can play in living things. An entire industry in the treatment of heart disease through pacemakers has resulted, and Earl Bakken has become a classic example of how being new-minded can make a profound difference in a person's life.

New-minded people like Earl Bakken often seem to have an inner compulsion that impels them to make the world a better place. This special trait seems to carry them from project to project and can be applied to any part of our human condition crying out for improvement. Indeed, if the need is great enough, it sometimes seems to attract new-minded people right out of the blue who bring with them the solutions that are so badly needed.

Take hospitals for example. Have you ever wondered why so often our healing institutions are such cold and impersonal places? Why so many seem to be "warehouses for the sick" with few of the touches of comfort or appealing surroundings that we take for granted in restaurants, hotels, public places, and our own homes? Isn't there a desperate need for new-minded thinking to bring about a "healing environment" that would reduce our fears of a hospital stay and, instead, trigger the power of the mind in healing the body?

Of course there is. However it took a whole team of new-minded thinkers to do something about it. This miracle, and it is a kind of miracle, took place in the nineties in the State of Hawaii.

Imagine the dream hospital that a group of new-minded strategic thinkers could create in Hawaii if they began with the goal of creating the finest healing facility possible. This hospital would take on a visual quality that would be exciting for both patients and hospital staff. In this Hawaiian setting, every room would be larger than usual and would have a door leading to the outside and sometimes to herbal gardens and waterfalls. Color schemes would be soft and muted with indigenous Hawaiian patterns and designs throughout to help the local patients feel at home. Patients would select the artwork that would hang in their room from the hospital art cart. This would allow them to change their artwork to suit the different moods they inevitably experience as the healing process takes place. According to their tastes, patients in each room would select their own music and videos. Hospitals would provide information on the healing aspects of laughter inspired by comedy as exemplified by Norman Cousins' experience in his best selling book, *Anatomy of an Illness.*

There would be many windows and natural light in every room of the building. Even the five surgical suites would have natural light with windows that could be darkened when certain surgical procedures required it. Patients would not be subjected to the usual hospital smells because of a state-of-the-art ventilation system. Skilled chefs would create healthy meals using local fish, fruit, and vegetables. There would be tranquil flower gardens, enhanced by flowing water, here and there throughout the grounds. These inviting spots would allow patients to sit and enjoy the therapy of nature as part of their healing process. There would be a prayer room in the hospital. All of the religions practiced locally would be included and it would serve as a real "center of hope". Such a hospital would be a center of mental, emotional, physical and spiritual healing, as well as a source of pride for the community it serves.

Today this dream hospital is a reality. It is Earl Bakken's latest project, and a perfect example of how new-minded thinking can be applied to any part of our lives requiring change. In 1990, Earl retired from Medtronic and moved to Hawaii. His new home is located on a beautiful beach on the west corner of the Big Island. Shortly after his arrival, a community group approached him about providing leadership for improving health and wellness for the twenty nine thousand people who live in the northwest corner of the island, an area called Kamuela.

Characteristically, Earl Bakken saw another opportunity to make a huge difference in the lives of others. The health statistics for this particular area were the worst in the state of Hawaii. Although there was a hospital on the island, it was located too far away to serve the northern part of the island effectively. There was no preventative care program for the people of the area. Bakken saw the need to turn a local dream into reality through building a very special hospital that would bring together experts from around the world in a collaborative effort to improve the art of healing. While in theory retired, Bakken agreed to provide leadership for the group in building what would eventually be called the North Hawaii Community Hospital and improving health care in the area.

One of the first steps in the process of making the

dream of a hospital a reality was to create a mission statement worded as follows. "The mission of the North Hawaii Community Hospital is to improve the health status of the people of North Hawaii by improving access to care and providing appropriate high quality services at a reasonable cost."

At the time the mission statement was created, there was little reason to believe that the hospital of their dreams could ever become a reality. There had been talk of such a hospital for sixty years, but it never got beyond talk. The writing of such a mission statement gave the group focus and purpose and the belief that the hospital could be built. In 1932 for the purpose of building a sanitarium Lucy Kalanikumaikiekie Henriques had bequeathed a twelve-acre site to the community. This was an ideal place for a hospital, but there was no building permit and no money. There was also a belief that physicians would not leave successful practices in areas that presented much more opportunity for top-notch doctors. Needed was new-minded thinking that could result in a vision capable of stirring the passions of the leadership group.

From the beginning the strategy team led by Bakken dreamed big dreams. The vision was to create a hospital unlike any other in the world, a place where every detail of the hospital experience would contribute to healing and a sense of well being. Earl Bakken put it this way, *"At North Hawaii Community Hospital, we have a golden opportunity to start a patient-oriented hospital from scratch."* The old rules would be thrown out and the facility would be built around the most important component of healing: the patient.

DIAMONDS

According to an article by Susan Pueschel, director of development for the hospital, *"At NHCH we are trying to create an environment wherein the people of the hospital work in partnership with the patients and their families, seeking peace of mind and peace of heart as well as physical cures and physical comfort. We do this because we're beginning to understand, through hard research and data, that there is an invisible relationship that exists between the body, the mind, and the mystery of life that we call spirit."*

On May 21, 1995, the people of the communities to be served by the new hospital gathered together to celebrate its dedication. The money had been raised through a combination of state grants and public donations. The building permit had been "earned" through spirited and dedicated efforts of the community group. The talented staff had been recruited, hired, and trained to treat patients with a loving concern that any of us would welcome, if we needed hospital care. The building was constructed, just as the dream had required and the mission demanded.

One extremely important aspect of the North Hawaii Community Hospital is the philosophy that guides and directs the nursing care. The concept of "the healing touch" is widely used, and nurses are certified in guided imagery, affirmations, the importance of words, and the healing power of laughter. In addition, consultants are available in chiropractic, homeopathy, massage therapy, herbal medicine, biofeedback, and acupuncture. Here is a hospital built by new-minded people that is open to all of the options that can aid and strengthen the healing process.

NEW-MINDEDNESS

Earl Bakken is living proof of the power of mission and new-minded thinking. Several months after the dedication, Earl gave us a tour of the new hospital. As he walked around the hospital that he helped create, there was a spring in his step, a pride in what had been accomplished, and a gleam in his eye as he saw the beauty that had been created. It was evident that one of the Diamonds had been at work here.

Leadership was the key to success in creating the North Hawaii Community Hospital. It is also crucial in corporate affairs. New-minded thinking in leadership was also present when Bill George addressed the Greater Minneapolis Chamber of Commerce with a talk entitled "The Soul of Your Corporation." George is a man with a very new-minded way of leading a major corporation. His belief is that the people at Medtronic, and elsewhere for that matter, do not work just for money or for career success, but for purpose. His talk at the Chamber meeting was a stimulating call to other corporate leadership to re-think the role of the corporation. His message was that workers have to feel that their work makes a difference, so that through their work they have the opportunity to serve others.

In George's words, *"The last thirty years of my business lifetime have been characterized by corporations known for "layoffs, payoffs, write-offs and spin-offs. To many employees, this has become a real "turnoff". People are really questioning what is their role in corporate life, the purpose they thought they signed up for ten, twenty, or thirty years ago. Those values in many corporations seem to have faded and seem to have changed. Many employees and even executives feel like they have had the rug pulled out from under them as the things they devoted their life and career to all of a sudden go away. I believe those of us in responsible positions in corporate management really have to take these concerns very, very seriously."*

You may be wondering what the impact of this new-minded approach to corporate leadership has been on the value of Medtronic stock. Over the past ten years the stock has appreciated an average of 37% a year. Investors have been well rewarded indeed by investing in new-minded leadership.

Walt Disney was a man who knew something about dreams and new-mindedness. He is thought of as the father of animated films that entire families could enjoy together. His films became popular during the tough economic times of the 1930's when people needed uplifting entertainment. His work was rewarded with forty eight Academy Awards and seven Emmys for art and entertainment excellence. Disney was a dreamer and a doer who once said, *"All our dreams come true, if we have the courage to pursue them."*

Yet Disney experienced his share of setbacks. His first attempt at drawing for publication was rejected and accompanied by a note telling him he had no artistic talent. His business schemes took him to the brink of bankruptcy on more than one occasion. His success was by no means either automatic or certain as he was finding his way in life.

But he was a man of dreams, and he kept on dreaming.

Disney used to take his daughters to a local park to play on Saturday afternoons and to ride the merry-go-round. It was at the park that he dreamed of an exceptional amusement park that one day would become Disneyland. His dreams were complete with The Pirates of the Caribbean, A Small, Small World, and Main Street USA. Disney was a visionary who was courageous enough to do whatever was necessary to turn his dreams into reality. He created his future by using his mind to see a future that was not visible to anyone else. He was a new-minded thinker.

In the business world we often see examples of people who need to become new-minded. Stuck in their own reality of business as usual, they are unable to bring about change. They know that their competition has become stronger, their products have become dated, and their operating systems no longer meet the needs of their people, yet they are unable to imagine a better way of doing things. With each passing day, they and their companies move closer to the brink of disaster. It is only when new-minded thinking is applied by seeing things as they could be, and imagining the resources of the organization applied more creatively, that positive change begins to take place. Struggling organizations often lack that one essential asset: new-minded thinking.

Diamonds look at life differently through the powerful eye of their imaginations as they search for creative solutions. They tend to be new-minded thinkers who consciously cultivate their imaginations through reading, listening to tapes and by surrounding themselves with other highly imaginative people.

What does this mean to people who have not become new-minded? It means that if you are not purposefully using your imaginations, if you are not dreaming exciting dreams of what the future could hold for you and your company, you probably have significantly limited your future. Robert Collier put it well: "The great successful men of the world have used their imaginations...they think and create their mental picture, and then go to work materializing that mental picture in all of its details, filling in here, adding a little there, building – steadily building."

Failure to be new-minded can prove embarrassing over time, especially if our position is quoted and comes back to haunt us at a later date. Newsweek Magazine in January of 1997 printed a review of predictions made by "visionaries" of times past who were in a position to have a new-minded view of the future and missed the boat:

"The horse is here to stay, but the automobile is only a novelty, a fad." A president of the Michigan Savings Bank advising Horace Rackam, (Henry Ford's lawyer), not to invest in the Ford Motor Company, 1903.

"Everything that can be invented has been invented." Charles Duell, U.S. commissioner of patents, 1899.

"What use could this company make of an electrical toy?" Western Union president William Orton, rejecting Alexander Graham Bell's offer to sell his struggling telephone company to Western Union for $100,000.

"Television won't be able to hold on to any market

it captures after the first six months. People will soon get tired of staring at a plywood box every night." Darryl F. Zanuck, head of 20th Century-Fox, 1946.

Diamonds consistently seek to meet new people. Knowing people with fresh ideas can help them achieve their goals faster than would otherwise be possible.

A network of talented, productive, innovative friends is an important asset for anyone. The key is to continually expand that network by seeking out people who have qualities, attributes, or just ideas with which you want to connect. It is very important to continually seek the stimulation and the diversity of thinking that accompanies new relationships. Verbalizing ideas with others can be a powerful tool. Possibilities that would never have come to you in a vacuum come easily in the ebb and flow of stimulating conversation. Many business leaders need a listener who can both debate and offer timely encouragement.

New-minded people seek out and adapt to new technology. All around us are tools to improve our productivity, our communications and our time management. Diamonds understand that adapting to changing technology is often the difference between prosperity and financial disaster. The learning curve we experience as we attempt to adapt to new technology is the price we pay for acceptable productivity.

New-Mindedness means a willingness to develop new habits to improve personal effectiveness, creativity, and well being. One way that Diamonds stay polished is by carefully selecting their habits and adding new habits as change dictates. It is the ability to select new habits that are right for each passage of life that allows Diamonds to remain Diamonds.

To sum it all up, a very special attribute of the people we call Diamonds is the ability to apply new-minded thinking in ways that improve their own lives and the lives of others. It is a great pathway to enhancing the most marvelous of all gifts, the gift of life itself. And this pathway is open to all of us.

DECISIVENESS

**Making timely decisions and acting
on them with firm determination.**

*"In any moment of decision the best thing you can do
is the right thing, the next best thing is the wrong
thing, and the worst thing that you can do is nothing"*
-Theodore Roosevelt-

The quality of decisiveness is critical to successful living, regardless of who we are or what we intend to do with our lives. Failure to make decisions or avoiding decisions is why so many people never achieve even a fraction of their potential.

The greatest single decision in World War II—and perhaps in the Twentieth Century—was contained in three words spoken quietly by an American officer with four stars on each of his shoulders. The time was June 1944. All around him, coiled like a gigantic spring, was one of the mightiest military forces ever assembled, more than two million soldiers, sailors and airmen, more than 6,000 ships, more than 14,000 warplanes. Month after month tension had been building in that spring. It would take one crucial decision by one man to release that power.

It was an agonizingly difficult decision. Outside, wind-driven rain swept over the green English countryside. Originally scheduled for June 4, the long-planned invasion of Nazi-held Europe was already running late. Further delay might rip the curtain of secrecy surrounding D-day and the element of surprise would be lost. On the other hand, weather conditions for a seaborne/airborne assault were miserable.

The man with the stars on his shoulders took one last look at the latest cautiously optimistic weather report that called for slightly better weather the following day. At last he glanced up at the group of officers surrounding him. *'Okay,'* said General Dwight D. Eisenhower with quiet finality, *'let's go.'*

In his Order of the Day to the men and women in his forces, the Supreme Commander wrote *'the hopes and prayers of liberty-loving people everywhere march with you.'* He also wrote, *'Your task will not be an easy one. Your enemy is well trained, well equipped and battle-hardened. He will fight savagely.'* Behind those words was a grim reality. The chance for success was marginal at best. The risk of failure was very high.

No one knew this better than Eisenhower. In his pocket that day was a message that he was prepared to make public if the Allied forces were driven back into the sea. It said that his decision to attack was based on the best information available. But it added that if the invasion failed, *'any fault or blame attached to the attempt is mine and mine alone.'*

Eisenhower's decision on June 5 was the turning point of the war. It makes one wonder where the capacity to make great decisions comes from. Is it based on a lifetime habit of making smaller ones? Perhaps Eisenhower's decisiveness had its origins far back in his childhood. His mother was a devout woman. 'The Lord deals the cards, Dwight,' she used to say. 'The way you play them is up to you.' As every card-player knows, each hand calls for a series of decisions, small ones perhaps, but crucial to the outcome of the game.

All through his military career Eisenhower faced hard decisions. Sometimes the decision was not to take action. The colorful (and difficult) British General, Bernard Montgomery, resented having to serve under Ike's command and made his feelings very plain. Eisenhower knew that with the backing of President Roosevelt he could have Montgomery assigned to a lesser position but his decision, in the interest of British-American relations, was to get along with him as best he could.

One glimpse of Eisenhower at the close of that fateful day gives us a hint of the awful loneliness of command and the responsibility that goes with it. Nightfall found the General at the air base where paratroopers of the 101st Airborne Division were awaiting the order to go. Just before dawn, as the long line of C-47s revved up their engines, Eisenhower stood on the roof of an administration building and saluted each plane as it thundered past. When the last one vanished into the murky darkness and he turned away, he had tears in his eyes.

Diamonds know that there are three components of decision-making that must be understood and mastered if success is to be achieved.

The first is **judgment**, a clear-minded assessment of all pertinent facts and the ability to weigh pros and cons and reach balanced conclusions.

The second is **timing**, the realistic perception that grasping the moment neither too soon nor too late is of the utmost importance in reaching desired goals.

The third is **integrity**, which includes the great intangibles: sensitivity to the moral implications of the decision, the courage to move forward without being deterred by the fear of failure, and the willingness—as in Eisenhower's message—to take responsibility for the outcome, good or bad, of events set in motion by the decision.

Armed with these three, decision-makers can move mountains.

The attribute of decisiveness requires constant, disciplined preparation so that confident, timely, and correct decisions are possible. Jerry Seeman is one man whose job requires extraordinary decisiveness and preparation. He has two coveted Super Bowl rings, the prizes earned for refereeing two Super Bowls. However, he is more than one of the finest referees in the world. For the past eight seasons his job is Director of Officiating for the National Football League. Jerry and his professional one hundred and twelve person organization are responsible for seeing to it that the best possible officiating decisions are made in every one of the sixteen football games played weekly during the football season. The work of the NFL Director of Officiating and his team epitomizes the word decisiveness.

NFL officiating requires an encyclopedic knowledge of the rules of the game, the fitness of an athlete, and the ability to make tough decisions instantly and correctly. All of this while looking over your shoulder are several million fans, who have the advantage of seeing the replay on their television screens.

Seeman has been an athlete, leader and role model for others since he was a boy growing up in the small farming community of Plainview, Minnesota. His high school football coach, Jerry Eckstein, remembers him as a natural leader, a quarterback who prepared diligently for games and was able to make many key decisions right on the field. "It was like having another coach," Coach Eckstein reminisces, "a smart, confident athlete that the other players looked up to. You don't get many like Jerry Seeman."

Seeman earned his current position through being personally decisive and through commitment to a program of continual improvement for both himself and his entire organization. The NFL officials training program that Seeman has developed is a model for organizational effectiveness and reflects the dedication of the man to his work. However, Jerry is quick to point out, *"I don't consider it work. It's my vocation and my love."*

Talking with Seeman, you get the impression that he

has always set high standards for himself. The decisions that he has made, his personal determination, and his constant preparations for success have made him a standout throughout his career. In high school and college, he was an outstanding student with a love of mathematics and sports. His first career was teaching, which led to a position in administration in the Fridley, Minnesota School system. At the same time, Seeman was working his way up the officiating ranks by refereeing high school games, then small college, then big college, until he finally was accepted as an official in the NFL.

The preparation on a year-round basis is significant. It begins on April 1 when the one hundred and twelve officials are given a course in the new rules that come out of the owners' meeting in March. Thorough testing is done in both April and May so that these new rules are absorbed. During the spring they visit the training camps and communicate with coaches and players. In July there is a clinic for the officials in which there is a stress test and rigorous physical exam. Again they go to training camps and communicate with coaches, players and among themselves. They study a pre-season training tape of forty to fifty plays tailored for their learning.

The objective, of course, is for every one of the referees to be both accurate and decisive in their officiating. As Seeman puts it: *"You're only as good as your last call. and your next. You have to concentrate very hard. You can never anticipate a call."* To encourage excellence every NFL official receives a packet each week from league headquarters in New York pertaining to the game he officiated the prior week. In the packet are videotapes of the game from every conceivable angle, a written test reinforcing officials' knowledge of the rules, and reams of written material to use in upgrading skills and to provide feedback. Each officiating crew meets additionally on the Saturday afternoon prior to their next officiating job to review a special customized forty five minute version of the videotapes from their last game. This tape is edited by Seeman and assistants to point out strengths and weaknesses of the crew, along with recommendations for improvement. It is the responsibility of the official to absorb all of this information so that the decisions made in their next game will be as good as they can possibly be. As the season comes to an end the top eleven officials are chosen for post season play.

Sometimes despite all the preparation the decisions of the officials are not as good as they can possibly be. Human beings are involved, and none of us is perfect, even if that is expected of us. Many of the problems that come up occur when split second decisions are in error, or the official is blocked from seeing the play properly. With over twenty two hundred plays a week, an uproar from players, coaches, owners and fans can arise as a result of just a few plays.

Unfortunately, over the years, incorrect calls by the officials have affected the outcomes of games. At the late winter owners' meeting in 1999, instant replay—the use of television replays to review officials' calls—returned for the '99 season after being away for seven years.

Dan Rooney, owner of the Pittsburgh Steelers, said: "I think the officials do a tremendous job, but this is something to help."

The new more limited instant replay format provides that each team receives two chances to challenge an official's call. If the team making the challenge is wrong it loses a timeout, and it has only three in each half. If a team is out of timeouts, it cannot challenge.

In speaking of the new rule, Jerry Seeman said, *"this is not an all encompassing system; it's the type of system that helps out, that tries to take TV replays and turn them into a positive. It's being used on a limited basis, and it's not obtrusive."*

Despite decisions gone wrong, what Jerry Seeman and his organization have created is a blueprint for developing the quality of decisiveness. It is a combination of education, preparation, practice, feedback, and the habit of making decisions in a timely fashion. Now it's true that the rest of us don't have to make split second decisions with millions of volatile fans watching, but we do have to know when a decision should be made, and be prepared to make those decisions. Every one of us can learn to be more decisive. The benefits to us personally and to our organizations would be enormous if each of us worked a little harder on this quality.

For Dr. Martin Luther King, Jr. decisiveness was a lifelong habit that took him from a middle-class upbringing in Atlanta to the pinnacle of the American civil-rights movement. When King came to prominence, being black meant living with injustice, hatred and prejudice. A true American hero, King fought his entire life for civil rights for all Americans and the elimination of segregation in the South. King once said, while watching tapes of the Kennedy assassination on television, *"I don't think I'm going to live to be forty. This is what's going to happen to me also."* Yet he was a determined man and totally committed to his decision to make a difference in the lives of others through the civil-rights movement.

As a college student King had been influenced by the success of Gandhi, who had brought about social change in India through non-violent protest. King thought that a similar approach might work for African Americans fighting racism in the United States. *"I've seen the hate on the faces of too many bigots to want to hate, because every time I see it, I know that it does something to their personalities, and I say to myself that hate is too great a burden to bear."* Instead, King had made a decision to base his life on love.

In spite of physical attacks, bombings of his home and over fifty threats on his life over a ten-year period, Martin Luther King, Jr. was determined to do whatever he could to open the minds of those inflamed by prejudice, hatred and intolerance. *"Courage faces fear and thereby masters it,"* was King's response to those who attempted to dissuade him from his role in the movement.

The night before King's assassination he once again affirmed his decision on how he chose to spend his life. In his final speech he said: *"We got some difficult days ahead. But it doesn't matter to me now. Because I have been to the mountaintop. And I don't mind. Like anybody, I would like to live a long life, but I'm not concerned with that now. I just want to do God's Will. And He's allowed me to go up to the mountain. And I've looked over. And I've seen the Promised Land. And I may not get there with you. But I want you to know tonight that we as a people will get to the Promised Land. And I'm happy tonight. I'm not worried about anything. I'm not fearing any man. Mine eyes have seen the glory of the coming of the Lord."* The late Senator Paul Douglas referred to Gandhi, Pope John XXIII and Dr. King as "the outstanding religious leaders of the century."

The decision to serve by Martin Luther King, changed the fabric of our society. Since January 15, 1983, King's birthday has been recognized as a national holiday in America. It is a good day to reflect on his words: *"We must learn to live together like brothers. or perish as fools."*

Effective decision making requires a sense of urgency, a belief that there is a correct time to make a decision. At Medtronic, Kristine Johnson's decision-making skills became very apparent. *"One of her greatest gifts,"* a colleague says, *"is her ability to ask penetrating questions. Right in the middle of a discussion, she has a way of posing a question that cuts to the heart of an issue and focuses people on what is important. She doesn't let people wander around in the forest."*

"I'll plead guilty to that," Kristine Johnson says. *"People tend to wrestle too long with decisions. This takes time and energy and slows down the process. The key is to sort through to the decision that really*

matters. It is also important to know which decisions can be reversed, so that fear of trying new or different ideas is minimized."

Asked about difficult decisions that she has made over the years, two came quickly to Kristine's mind. The first occurred in the early years of the defibrillator business. Medtronic ranked somewhere in the middle of companies pursuing this market. The clock was ticking, as the leading companies in the race concentrated on putting great distance between themselves and pursuers like Medtronic. A problem arose with the Medtronic defibrillators and, as these were implantable devices, the integrity of the product was paramount. Kristine made the decision to stop clinical testing in order to correct the problem. They did this and made the necessary modifications. It was a difficult decision that had a short-term negative impact on the program. As Kris reflects today, she feels that in the end it was overly conservative. At the time though, she did what she felt was the right thing to do. She made the decision.

Another situation requiring decisiveness that Kris recalls involved Bill Heilan, a long-time highly valued Medtronic co-worker. As General Manager, when the Tachyarythmic Division was in its early stages, Kris knew she needed an experienced manufacturing leader who could gear the division to a high level of excellence. Bill Heilan had that reputation with the Brady Pacemaker Division of Medtronic. In the eyes of some people it would have been a step backwards for Bill to become Director of Manufacturing in the fledgling Tachyarythmic Division. Further complicating the

situation was the fact that Bill Heilan had been bat-
tling cancer.

Bill and Kristine knew that although the cancer was in
remission, there was no guarantee as to how long that
would continue. Still, after careful thought and discussion, the job was offered and Bill accepted. He played
a superb role in establishing the foundation for manufacturing a very high quality product. When Bill's cancer returned, Kris met the challenge of managing
around Bill's reduced work time, and ultimately had to
decide if Bill should stay in his job. According to Kris,
this was the "real learning time" for her and the whole
team. Despite Bill's cancer, she made the decision to
keep Bill in his position. Others, including Kris, needed to take up the slack, and they did.

This decision was one of those delicate balancing acts
where what is right for the individual has to be balanced
with what is right for the company. Even though Bill's
increasingly frequent absences put more pressure on
everyone, the team grew because of it. Kris was keenly aware that a decision in favor of the individual could
be very costly for the company and many others within
the company. Bill has since passed away, but Kris felt
at the time that her decision to leave him in the job was
the right thing to do. They succeeded because of the
team's uncommon commitment.

Kristine once said, *"Part of lifelong learning is
doing things, making choices and not being afraid of
making choices. It is not as much making right or
wrong decisions, as moving forward and making
adjustments."* It is this sense of decisiveness that sets
Kristine Johnson apart. To paraphrase Oliver Wendell

Holmes, she is sailing, not drifting—and definitely "not lying at anchor."

Diamonds understand that one of the most important decisions they ever make is what their life's work will be. Actor and producer Michael Landon became a famous TV star as "Little Joe" in Bonanza, "Pa" in Little House on the Prairie, and an "angel" in *Highway to Heaven*.

Landon grew up in New Jersey with the given name of Eugene Orowitz and the nickname of "Ugy". He was a shy, introverted tenth grader with no acknowledged athletic ability when the high school track coach noticed him watching the javelin competition. When asked if he would like to try, "Ugy" hurled the javelin beyond the field and into the stands, startling himself, the coach and everyone watching. He made the decision on the spot to excel in track competition with the javelin and backed the decision up with practice, night and day. "Ugy" did indeed excel by breaking the national high school record at that time for throwing the javelin. He won a track scholarship to college in California, and probably would have competed in the Olympics had not a torn shoulder muscle ended his track career.

When Landon's track career was over, he looked for something else and discovered acting. While helping a friend prepare for a part in a play, he was bitten by the dramatic bug and made a decision to enroll in Warner Brothers Acting School. The rest is history. Michael Landon, "Ugy", became one of the most respected performers of his generation. His decision to commit to quality work and inspirational family entertainment resulted in some of the best television entertainment of the past several decades. He was a man who made one good decision after another about the roles he accepted, and the projects he produced.

Diamonds have often paid the price of giving up security in the form of a regular paycheck for the adventure of doing what they really love to do. Some financial risk may be involved, but when a person does what he loves, it often follows that performance, productivity and results improve so much that the rewards just automatically follow.

Today experts agree that most of us, unlike prior generations, may experience a number of career changes during our lifetime. This gives each of us more than one chance to find our niche in the world. Many of us can afford to take more risks, and experiment with jobs we think might provide the challenges, rewards, and opportunities for self-actualization that we all want from our work.

The challenge is to stay aware of the possibilities and be an informed decision-maker when it comes to the choice of your next career.

Then have the courage to take a risk, move forward and try living your dream.

SERVICE

Helping others with a deep sense of caring, gives meaning and fulfillment to life.

"I don't know what your destiny will be, but one thing I do know, that the only ones among you who will be really happy, are those among you who have sought and found how to serve."
-Dr. Albert Schweitzer-

The seven chapters that precede this one are devoted to a set of qualities that can indeed contribute dramatically to the splendor of living. Desire, Integrity, Attitude, Mission, Openness, New-Mindedness and Decisiveness are like facets of a diamond that can be polished and made to sparkle with brilliant intensity.

But in the long run, what is the ultimate purpose of applying the self-discipline and persistence it takes to develop these qualities? Is it simple self-improvement? Or is it something much deeper? The answer can be found in the words of Dr. Schweitzer quoted above. The truly successful, the truly happy human being is the one who has learned to serve.

This is a skill that cannot be acquired overnight. Some people never master it. All of us start out in life preoccupied with our own needs and hopes and desires, a self-centeredness characteristic of all living creatures. Describing his studies of the basic element of life, the single cell, Dr. Hans Selye, the great authority on stress, puts it like this: "The cell has a quality that it shares with all living things, the quality of self-centeredness. There is no doubt that it is the instinct and perhaps the obligation of every organism to look out for itself. Call it self-preservation, selfishness, or what you will, it's built into all of us."

Fortunately, even if we start out caring mainly about ourselves, we don't have to stay this way. The long journey from self-caring to caring about others is a challenge that confronts us every day of our lives. And the farther we progress in the journey, the more apparent it becomes that to improve in each of the qualities discussed in this book is to improve our ability to serve in our jobs, our marriages, our communities, in all the many facets of life that surround us.

When we apply the lessons of the preceding seven chapters of this book to the service of others, that is when "living with splendor" begins.

There is a word for people who touch the lives of others in a significant way. That word is "mentor". Mentoring is a caring service that rewards both the mentor and the recipient. By definition a mentor is a wise and trusted counselor. We all need such people in our lives. By sharing their insights and listening carefully, they may help remove an obstacle in someone's path. When this happens, both parties usually leave the experience with their lives enriched.

Mentors played an important role in the life of Reatha Clark King. Says Reatha, *"My mentors were very special."* Many people, parents, family and friends played a part in encouraging Reatha along her educational path. However, in her early years at Clark College in Atlanta, there were two who were especially timely in Reatha's life.

During Reatha's first year at Clark, the Dean of Women, Phoebe Hart, guided her to a summer job with the Harvey Dann family of Pawling, New York. It was there that Lois Dann entered Reatha's life as a second mother with her warmth, thoughtfulness and ability to share. It was Reatha's job over the next four summers to help care for the three children, Mary, Tyler and Harvey. The impact of Lois Dann on Reatha's personal growth was immeasurable. She had the emotional stability to avoid making a crisis out of anything, a characteristic that you see reflected in the calm demeanor of Reatha Clark King today.

Lois was a very caring mentor to Reatha. Norman Vincent Peale, who lived in Pawling, saw the remarkable nurturing capacity in Lois Dann, and said to her one day, "Lois, you must be the best mother in the whole world." Lois helped Reatha map out weekly sightseeing trips to New York City where Reatha felt the thrill of her world opening up around her.

Mentoring is a special service. The feeling of having made a genuine difference in the life of someone you care for is payment in full. The service given by teachers is often critical in helping students discover their unique skills and aid them in finding personal satisfaction in their life's work.

When Reatha started at Clark in the fall of 1954 she felt, *"the faculty was determined to make something out of each of us."* One of those faculty members was Dr. Alfred Spriggs, Chairman of the Chemistry Department. Reatha originally planned to study Home Economics and return home to teach. Dr. Spriggs took an interest in Reatha and gently began widening her horizons. He encouraged her to be adventuresome. Gradually, Reatha looked increasingly to Dr. Spriggs for guidance, as his role became both that of teacher and mentor. It was not too surprising that her major changed to chemistry. The relationship of the teacher and student, the mentor and the protégé can create a special chemistry of its own. Dr. Spriggs gave her an understanding of what a research chemist is, and strengthened her confidence to proceed in a profession that was not considered very appropriate for a young woman at that time. Reatha explained that this support, coming from a man, was especially important to her. Some years later, in 1968, while working for the National Bureau of Standards, Reatha won her division's Outstanding Publication Award for a research paper on oxygen difluoride. Somewhere Dr. Spriggs had to be smiling.

SERVICE

One of the greatest examples of service in the twentieth century is the story of Helen Keller and her teacher and life-long companion, Anne Sullivan Macy. Helen was only six when she first met Anne. From that day onward, Anne saw the development of Helen Keller as her supreme mission. *"The education of this child will be the distinguishing event of my life."*

Today we think of Helen Keller as one of the heroines of the twentieth century, a woman who overcame the disabilities of deafness and blindness to become an inspiration for all of us. When we think of Helen Keller, we think of courage and achievement. We remember her words that summarize her philosophy of life, *"Security is mostly a superstition. It does not exist in nature, nor do the children of men as a whole experience it. Avoiding danger is no safer in the long run than outright exposure. Life is either a daring adventure or nothing."*

For over forty four years Helen Keller worked as an advocate of human rights for the blind. She became a famous author and public speaker, but she also had a well-developed sense of humor. None of this would have been possible without Anne Sullivan. When asked if women are men's intellectual equals Helen replied, *"I think God made woman foolish so that she might be a suitable companion to man."*

Helen Keller was born in the village of Tuscumbia, Alabama, June 27, 1880. In February of 1881 an undiagnosed disease accompanied by a very high fever left the child deaf and blind. In later years, she would say that her months of "light", before being stricken, were an advantage because she had seen grass, sky, sun and had begun the development of her personality which is so important in the first two years of life. Helen refers to herself as *"a wild, uncouth little creature"* before Anne came to her.

Helen's father, a former officer in the Confederate Army, employed Anne Sullivan as a teacher and companion to Helen in 1887 when Helen was six years old. "I would be willing to give Miss Sullivan her board, washing, etc., and twenty-five dollars per month and we would treat her as one of our immediate family," he wrote to the director of Perkins Institution for the Blind in Boston where he hoped to find a governess for the child.

In her autobiography, *The Story of My Life*, the first meeting of Anne Sullivan, and her blind and deaf pupil was described by Helen Keller. *"I felt approaching footsteps, I stretched out my hand as I supposed to my mother. Someone took it, and I was caught up and held close in the arms of her who had come to reveal all things to me, and more than all things else, to love me."* Anne Sullivan speaks of her impressions of that meeting, *"I remember how disappointed I was when the untamed little creature stubbornly refused to kiss me, and struggled to free herself from my embrace. I remember, too, how her eager, impetuous fingers felt my face and dress and my bag which she insisted on opening at once, showing by signs that she expected to find something good to eat in it."* It was March 3, 1887. For the rest of her life Helen Keller would celebrate this date as *"her soul's birthday"*.

From the beginning, Anne attempted to communicate with Helen by spelling out the letters of words into Helen's hand. The great break-through in Helen's education came on a day when she was walking with Anne by a well-house on the Keller property. As Helen relates the story, *"as the cool stream gushed over one hand, she (Annie) spelled into the other the word 'water,' first slowly, then rapidly. I stood still, my whole attention fixed upon the motion of her fingers. Suddenly I felt a misty consciousness as of something forgotten...a thrill of returning thought; and somehow the mystery of language was revealed to me. I knew that W-A-T-E-R meant the wonderful cool something that was flowing over my hand. I left the well-house eager to learn. Everything had a name, and each name gave birth to a new thought. As we returned to the house, every object which I touched seemed to quiver with life."*

The experience at the well-house became the stuff of legend, a miracle according to Anne. *"She has learned that everything has a name and that the manual alphabet is the key to everything she wants to know. Helen got up this morning like a radiant fairy. She has flitted from object to object, asking the name of everything and kissing me for very gladness. Last night when I got into bed, she stole into my arms of her own accord and kissed me for the first time, and I thought my heart would burst, so full was it of joy."* Using the technique of spelling out words in Helen's hand, Anne was able to teach Helen the meaning of three hundred words within a matter of months and continued to teach her five to six new words each day. Helen became so excited by the stimulation of learning and communicating that she could barely eat or sleep. According to Anne, *"At this point in Helen's development, she begins to spell the minute she wakes up in the morning and continues all day long. If I refuse to talk to her, she spells into her own hand, and apparently carries on the liveliest conversations with herself."*

Anne Sullivan had accomplished marvelous things with Helen Keller in the first four months of becoming her mentor and teacher. The story goes that when Queen Victoria personally presented Helen Keller with one of England's highest awards, she asked two questions: *"How do you account for your remarkable accomplishments in life?"* and, *"How do you explain the fact that even though you were blind and deaf, you were able to accomplish so much?"* Without a moment's hesitation, Helen Keller replied, *"If it had not been for Anne Sullivan, the name Helen Keller would have remained unknown."*

One of our greatest opportunities for service is inside our own family. As husband or wife, parent or sibling, you can make a difference every day in the lives of your family members. Patty and Tom Holloran started doing this early in their relationship. Like others who are separated by distance, they wrote to each other every day while Tom was in the Navy during the Korean War. Tom speaks with great warmth of Patty's being there for him in his various endeavors.

They have a remarkable capacity for focusing on each other's needs. Patty remembers long discussions with Tom in 1967 when he was considering leaving his law firm for the position of Executive Vice President at Medtronic. She and their two daughters Mary and Anne, who were ten and eight, would be facing a different kind of life. Tom would be traveling much more in his new position, and personal sacrifices would need to be made. Sensing what it meant to Tom, she gave him her loving support.

Perhaps Tom and Patty's secret in accomplishing so much together is found in Patty's definition: "Home is a place where you go to be refreshed." A deeply caring relationship allows two people to focus on each other and enjoy the close bonding that sustains each partner. Patty says appreciatively, "When Tom is home he's home. He doesn't let things bother him." Simple acts of support and encouragement to family members represent a meaningful service that is a vital part of human existence and fulfillment.

The roles of parent and grandparent are among the most rewarding and satisfying of all of life's experiences. It is by communicating a sense of caring in family relationships that a deposit is made in what Stephen Covey calls the "emotional bank account." It is a series of these deposits made during the formative years of your children and grandchildren that may be remembered with deep appreciation as long as they live.

Regardless of your vocation, treating your co-workers as you would like to be treated is at the heart of good relationships with them. It is one of the highest forms of service to others.

DIAMONDS

When Elmer Andersen became President of H.B. Fuller in 1941 his mission was two-fold. He wanted to make the company grow and he also wanted to create an attractive working environment for his co-workers. To Elmer, *"the secret to good relationships is to provide an environment where people can be at their best, one that helps people achieve their potential."* In his first annual report, Elmer noted, *"there have been few changes in personnel and relations among all the people of our organization are excellent."* He established a culture where the organization was of service to its workers.

In 1944, to celebrate his tenth year at Fuller, Elmer gave each employee two extra weeks of vacation and five hundred dollars. His instructions were brief: *"Go have fun. No house painting. No car payments."* Then in 1945 he inaugurated the idea of giving each of his employees their birthday as an extra personal holiday. *"We were a close-knit company. We cared about each other."* From the beginning Elmer's philosophy was: *"It has to be fun. You're in business to serve."* For Elmer Andersen of H.B. Fuller Company, that included serving your co-worker.

Speaking as Chairman of the company many years later to one hundred and fifty salespeople, Elmer described the corporate culture of H.B. Fuller. *"What we have been trying to do all these years is to build a company with an existence, a personality, a character, and an integrity all its own. We are each part of the Fuller family. We work together, we have a common purpose, and a common interest. We care about people."*

SERVICE

Over the years, Fuller's commitment to their co-workers led to an expansion of their benefits package to include not only pension plans and medical and dental benefits, but also life insurance and tuition payments. Elmer was never completely satisfied. One day he was reviewing the problems a St. Paul plant worker was having because his retirement benefits were not enough. Before long Elmer came up with a new set of comprehensive benefits plus a liberalized vacation policy that he explained to employees via videotape in a fireside chat style. This honest and open message had an affirmative rippling effect throughout the entire company.

The vacation policy was classic Elmer. Co-workers could hold over one week's vacation time and add it to the following year. On the tenth anniversary of their employment and every five years thereafter, they were awarded two weeks bonus time and an eight hundred dollar after-tax payment. The vacation policy, like many other ideas, was the legacy of Elmer Andersen. He believed that if Fuller people wanted to see the world, they should have the time and the opportunity to do so.

In 1984, H.B. Fuller was named to the Fortune 500 based on its 1983 performance. It also marked the celebration of Elmer Andersen's fiftieth year with the company. On that occasion marking the distinctive service of both the man and the company, Elmer was very clear about the company's philosophy, *"Very early, I felt that a corporation was a privileged organization, and that a company owed society two things: to do as well as it could in providing services to its customers, and to share the fruits of its rewards with its employees. At Fuller, we've always tried to do those two things."*

DIAMONDS

When asked at the time to identify challenges for Fuller in the future Elmer thought carefully and said, *"One of our biggest challenges remains communication among ourselves. That means taking time and energy to keep employees informed. It means working to build mutual confidence, trust and teamwork that gives a company strength. If people realize it is the quality of human relationships that is the most important, not the plants, research or growth, then the rest will take care of itself."*

Living in service to our friends requires sensitivity to their situation and the realization that good relationships require good communication. Over many decades James P. Shannon has been a valued friend to many people in the Twin Cities and elsewhere. For the better part of twenty years Jim wrote a weekly column for the *Minneapolis Tribune* on a wide variety of topics. It was a sterling feature of the paper, and Jim developed a substantial following.

Jim Shannon is a warm friendly man of sturdy build. His attentive eyes and relaxed demeanor make for easy conversation. He touches the lives of many people, in part because he is there for other people when they need him. His conviction that *"Service to other people is the milk of the coconut"*, is the way that he lives. He says, *"I carefully try not to be intrusive. I try to be responsive to them, and available when they call."*

Jim has some interesting views on the subject of friendship. When asked about close friends, he said, *"I don't think that we can afford more than six. You're making a long-term contract of your psychic capital when you invest in true friendship."* Jim calls it *"the inner circle of your soul-mates."* You may not have seen one of these friends for a long time, but when you make contact, *"the old magic is still there."*

An important part of service in relationships with friends is staying in touch. Without some effort it is easy to lose contact with one's friends. Many years ago Jim acquired an idea from a friend that helps him bridge this gap. Each day he cuts items from newspapers or periodicals that he feels might be of interest or help to someone he knows. Jim jots a personal note to go with the clipping. He averages close to ten a day. This practice keeps the lines of communication open to many of the people he cares about. Sometimes the result is a lengthy letter of reply and other times brief but valuable notes like, *"I'm healing. I'm ambulatory. I eat every day. How about you?"*

Everyone needs someone in their life who cares enough to be a sounding board. Jim Shannon feels that one of the greatest services that any of us can provide is just being available to listen. When we listen, we must also **hear**. *"Most of us miss a lot of clues that somebody else is hurting. Hearing is connecting. When you connect, you are caring at a deeper level."* Sometimes you are there to simply let the person unload and feel measurably better. Other times you are there to help brainstorm a problem for a solution. Discerning why you are there, and acting accordingly, requires a measure of wisdom. Diamonds have acquired this wisdom through awareness, practice and sensitivity to the needs of others. They have an abundance of meaningful relationships and friendships, because they practice the art of service to one another.

The opportunities of providing service to the community in which you live are around you every day. Here is how one person answered the call.

"Two years ago I was asked to Chair the United Way Campaign for Greater Minneapolis in 1997. My first reaction was to say 'No', I am not a good fundraiser. I don't have the time, I'm too committed elsewhere. But as I reflected on it, I realized that it was my turn to take the lead in the community. So I agreed, and have tried to bring a sense of caring about the kids in our community to the fund raising task. I learned also the tremendous commitment you can generate from others when you are very committed yourself. If not now, then when? If not me, then who? I do believe that part of all of our calling is to give back to the community or communities which helped launch us on our way." These were some informal remarks made by Bill George as he shared his thoughts on a variety of topics with some people in his church.

Before serving as Chairperson of the 1997 United Way campaign, Bill had been a dedicated volunteer for more than twenty years. During that summer he was leading Medtronic's participation in United Way's Week of Caring. This is an annual event that helps match more than 150 local companies and its people with volunteer projects. Bill was very involved either wielding a paintbrush during Project for Pride in Living's annual Paint-a-thon, or personally mentoring at-risk teens. In addition, he provided paid time off for more than 700 Medtronic co-workers, or roughly 20% of Medtronic's local workforce, to work on various volunteer projects. The United Way says Medtronic is the record holder for having the most employee volunteers on projects.

"It's in our mission statement to be a good corporate citizen," George says. *"I just think it's good for the company that we do some good out there. Personally, I think a week of caring is just scratching the surface."* When the United Way of Minneapolis announced its results for 1997, they had raised a total of $54 million or $3 million dollars more than the previous year. The United Way said that for the first time in many years they would be able to give more than a cost of living increase to those projects that benefit children, as well as others among the two hundred plus programs it supports each year.

Diamonds tend to give a great deal of themselves back to their communities. They see service to the community as a chance to "give back."

How do you balance the needs of your job with the need to provide service to your community? How do you find the hours your family expects from you when you are giving up your time to others?

Time is pretty unyielding stuff. Each of us has exactly the same amount of it, and we can't change that. What we can change is the way we look at time and how we use it.

The problem is partly mental. Many of us have the habit of thinking that one option blocks out another. Many of us have the habit of saying, "Oh, I don't have time for any more obligations; the ones I already have keep me fully occupied. Yes, I'd like to spend more time with my family, but my job is so demanding that there aren't enough hours in the day!"

This excuse may sound plausible, but in reality it's not. Your job may indeed be demanding, but almost certainly it could be done just as well in less time if you would learn to focus your efforts more effectively. Time may be unyielding in terms of minutes or hours, but it would seem to expand dramatically if you made a determined effort to increase efficiency and eliminate waste.

It's a little like packing a suitcase. Some people are much better packers than others. They are limited by the same cubic dimensions, but they don't just stuff items in at random, and they don't waste space. They anticipate the different bulk requirements of different garments and follow a logical progression in fitting them together. The result? Their suitcase carries twenty or thirty percent more than the identical cases of the haphazard packers.

And another thing. Many times it's possible to discover areas where two or more formerly separate activities can be carried on simultaneously without loss of effectiveness. People who learn how to 'blend' time in this fashion are often leaders in their communities and their professions.

Bill and Penny George believe in a strong family life, and they work together so this can happen. They have two sons, Jeff and Jon. Today, Jeff is twenty-five and in graduate school for advanced international studies in Baltimore. Jon, age twenty-two is a recent graduate of Amherst College in Massachusetts. Back in 1983 they were ten and seven and both were taking an interest in soccer. Having played high school football and college tennis, Bill admits that he didn't know too much about soccer. This lack of knowledge was short lived. He rounded up books and videos and *"started to learn soccer."*

When Bill began coaching in 1983, his first priority was their family. He and Penny would walk around the Lake of the Isles in Minneapolis where they lived whenever time permitted. On the weekends they tailored their social life around the family. There were no evening engagements, and Bill turned down breakfasts and lunches. There was no tennis. Bill was making a major commitment to his family, his co-workers and his soccer team members, and so was Penny. As a consulting psychologist, Penny appreciated the need for a closely-knit team, if she and Bill were to undertake the soccer involvement and fulfill their other commitments. For ten years she and Bill would have a late post-soccer Wednesday night dinner. The concept of serving is meaningful to Penny and for her it says that "my life has value, and it matters. I don't know of anything else that would do this."

After work each day Bill would pick up six to seven team members in his Chrysler van and by 5:30 all sixteen players were at practice. There were many company meetings when Bill had to depart early. *"When you've got a bunch of kids gathering on the field at 5:30, and you're trying to teach them something about discipline and responsibility, you'd better be there at 5:30."*

From April into August there would be five to six

practices or games a week consuming about twenty hours a week with approximately seventy games a year being played. Family dinners took place about 9:00 p.m. Bill took his team to out of town tournaments, with some traveling to France, Holland, Russia and Sweden. Then there were the return visits. One was the first Russian soccer team ever to play in the United States. Another time visiting Swedish players stayed with members of Bill's team. To accomplish the necessary preparation and execution of a seventy-game season required an additional five to six hours per week during the winter months. It was a tremendous commitment of time and energy by two caring people.

During Bill's thirteen years of coaching, his teams won four state championships, and finally in 1995, after eight tries, the prestigious International USA Cup Tournament. Great as that record is, the real story is the incalculable service Bill and Penny gave to those young soccer team members over thirteen years, including their two sons.

The rewarding aspect about Bill's investment of time is the degree of enjoyment and fulfillment that he experienced. Service to family and community almost always is that way, but it does take some creativity and desire to make it all work as it should.

DIAMONDS

And so we come to the end of our book believing that the eight key qualities of Diamonds are attainable. Of these eight qualities the most enduring and important is the final one: the challenge of service to others.

One of the most famous stories of all time was designed to hammer this point home. A great power that Jesus had was his ability to open the minds of his followers by using his storytelling skills. The parable that he chose in this case begins with the words, *"A certain man went down from Jerusalem to Jericho and fell among thieves."* With marvelous clarity and brevity, the story goes on to describe the victim left dazed and bleeding in the road. Along comes "a certain priest" who sees the injured man, but ignores him and goes away. Next comes a Levite, a member of a privileged class, who also "passes by on the other side." Finally, it is a Samaritan from a group of people not held in high regard, who not only stops and gives first aid, but also carries the victim to an inn and pays the innkeeper to take care of him. *"Which now of these three,"* Jesus asks his listeners, "was neighbor unto him who fell among thieves?"

The message is unmistakable: some people have a nobler sense of service than others. We owe it not just to the people we approve of, or who are a lot like ourselves, but to any one in need or in trouble, anywhere, any time.

If you can learn to keep this moral imperative in the forefront of your mind and heart, the door to the splendor of living will swing wide for you—always.

ACKNOWLEDGMENTS

Our warm thanks go to the people interviewed for this book, the majority of whom were seen more than once. At no time did we share with any of them the Diamonds concept. We told them only that we were writing a book about people of high integrity who were making a difference with their lives.

We would also like to thank those who helped us by reading the book at various stages of its development and offering their comments. Russ Bennett, John Butler, Voss Graham, Robin Graham, Ken Melrose, Jeff McGuinness, Dave Pemberton, Elizabeth Sherrill, and John Sherrill. All were an essential part of this effort.

Tucker Johnson was another ally, whose computer research uncovered vital information that otherwise would have remained unknown to us.

Dick Reid, the retired director of media relations at Medtronic, has been a valued friend with his gracious willingness to answer our many questions.

Another person who made a very substantial contribution was Bob Aulicino. His guidance in the jacket and book design was invaluable to us.

Finally we would like to offer a warm tribute to a very special lady. Diane Esterley was tireless in handling the various ideas that came from the authors for entry onto her computer diskette. She lived every moment of this book with us and made many valuable suggestions.

The aforementioned people gave willingly of their time, and we are most grateful to each of them.

BIBLIOGRAPHY

Anderson, Peggy, *Great Quotes From Great Leaders*, Lombard, Illinois: Celebrating Excellence Publishing, 1990

Carnegie, Dale, *Lincoln the Unknown*, Garden City, New York: Dale Carnegie & Associates, Inc.

Covey, Stephen, *The 7 Habits of Highly Effective People*, New York: Simon & Schuster, 1989

Davis, Wynn, *The Best of Success*, Lombard, Illinois: Celebrating Excellence Publishing, 1990

Gordon, Arthur, *Return to Wonder*, Nashville, Tennessee, Broadman & Hillman,1996

Griffith, Joe, *The Speaker's Library of Business Stories, Anecdotes and Humor*, Englewood Cliffs, New Jersey, Prentice Hall, 1990

Haskins, James, *The Life and Death of Martin Luther King, Jr.*, William Morrow & Company, 1992

Lash, Joseph, *Helen and Teacher*, Reading, Massachusetts, Addison Wesley Publishing Company, Inc., 1980

Leiman, Dan, *The Achievers*, St. Charles, Illinois: High Impact Products, Inc. 1994

Lewis, David, *King: A Biography*, University of Illinois Publishing, 1978

Olsen, Kermit R., *First Steps in Prayer*, Westwood, New Jersey: Fleming H. Revell Company, 1957

Pine & Mundale, Inc., *A Fuller Life*, copyright By H. B. Fuller Company, 1986

Sheehy, Gail, *Pathfinders*, New York, Bantam Books,1977

Shute, Evan, *The Vitamin E. Story*, Burlington, Ontario, Welch Publishing Company, 1985

Tracy, Brian, *Advanced Selling Strategies*, New York: Simon & Schuster, 1995